LEGAL GUIDELINES

FOR UNLICENSED

PRACTITIONERS

Dr. Lawrence Wilson

ISBN 0-9628657-2-9

Other books by Dr. Lawrence Wilson:

Nutritional Balancing and Hair Mineral Analysis
Healing Ourselves
Sauna Therapy
The Real Self

To order books and CDs, call 1(888) 330-6456 or visit www.drlwilson.com

TABLE OF CONTENTS

DEDICATION

I dedicate this book to all the great men and women who have fought to preserve the principles of individual liberty in America and around the world.

I also dedicate this book to my parents, Myron and Helen Wilson. It was they, more than anyone else, who helped me to learn critical thinking by challenging many of my ideas throughout childhood and as an adult as well. To them I say, thank you so much for teaching me to think clearly and logically.

INTRODUCTION

This book was written to spare you, dear reader, the confusion that I experienced as an unlicensed practitioner. I earned a medical degree in 1979. I left an internship early due to a health condition. As a result, I did not complete the requirements for licensure. For 32 years, I have elected to work as an unlicensed nutrition and lifestyle consultant. Several legal skirmishes arose related to an unlicensed status. I also watched many of my colleagues become embroiled in legal conflicts related to their holistic healing practices. I realized that I was better off than many of my licensed colleagues. The lessons learned are presented here.

This volume will assist anyone to understand the occupational licensing laws in order to work within the American and European system of laws. The intent is also to clarify legal and regulatory principles that served America well for over 120 years. These are the principles of free market economics, as applied to health care and to many other fields as well. These principles are quite simple. Some day, hopefully, this material will be taught in every high school.

Many gifted individuals are offering exciting and effective methods of therapy in the healing arts, psychology and other licensed professions. Occupational laws, however, often hinder rather than encourage these much-needed innovations. In fact, the trend at this time is to pass more laws for licensing professions. Whether intended or not, their effect is to reduce innovation and to protect often costly, outdated and toxic methods of treating mental and physical ailments.

The material in this book was originally compiled for natural healing practitioners. However, most of the principles and ideas it contains also apply to practitioners in education, psychology, and other professions as well. Also, while this book was written for those who are unlicensed, most of the material within it will benefit greatly the licensed practitioners as well.

The first half of the book contains common sense suggestions for safely conducting a practice. These range from words that should be avoided to simple safeguards such as disclosure, disclaimer and consent forms. The second half of the book delves into more detail about the occupational licensing laws, constitutional and other rights, and the Ninth Amendment.

PREMISES OF THIS BOOK

The premises of this book may seem a bit radical. The word radical means to go to the root cause. The Arizona State Constitution at Article II, 2, states: *"A frequent recourse to fundamental principles is essential to the security of individual rights and the perpetuity of free government."* With that in mind, let us begin with and never stray far from fundamental legal principles. Among these principles are:

1.*The sovereignty of the individual, rather than that of the government, is the basis for the American legal system.* This idea derives from the concept of natural rights. Natural rights are those that are God-given and antedate mankind's entrance into any society. Today they are often referred to as 'human rights'. No government should infringe upon them.

The concept of natural rights stems from the writings of the English philosopher John Locke, among others. He, along with other European political philosophers, heavily influenced the founders of the American nation. However, the idea can be traced all the way back to the biblical concept of divine laws that are to be held sacred above all man-made laws.

2. *Natural rights apply to individuals, and never to groups or organizations.* Among these are the rights to life, liberty and the pursuit of happiness. Laws and governments exist to help *each individual* achieve his or her highest potential. This is done by the government acting so as to protect each person's natural and other rights.

Today, this principle has been turned inside out. Governments often dictate what is best, rather than protecting the rights of all citizens to choose their own type of health care and education, and to make many other important decisions as well. Also, social classes, unions, occupational groups and industries today often receive government protection at the expense of individuals. Among the occupational groups are physicians, attorneys, teachers and others.

3. *The ability to heal others is a gift from the Creator, and a way of loving others. It is an ancient and natural human vocation. Current laws do not acknowledge this fact.* Instead, they place innumerable restrictions upon who can heal or educate another, and how it may be done, even if no harm comes to anyone.

I suggest in this book that this is the cause of the present health care and education problems that America and most other nations are experiencing. By restricting who works, and what methods they must use, many low-cost, safe and effective methods are denied the opportunity to be tested and incorporated into our health care, educational and other societal systems.

4. *The legal structure of the healing arts and the public education system are outdated and quite inadequate for the task of healing and educating all of humanity on every level of human functioning.* The system of occupational licensing laws gives control of health care, for example, to one group of practitioners. This stifles creativity, innovation and healthy competition.

However, due to the great need for healing today, these laws are, at times, not strictly enforced. The author's experience is that in many cases, an unlicensed person can practice many alternative therapies, provided your intent is pure and you follow certain procedures.

KEYS TO SUCCESS

- Always maintain high ethical standards. Accept complete responsibility for your situation and for your work.
- Understand the legal environment in which you live and where you work.
- Understand the belief systems or paradigms that operate in your field, especially those of the authorities, in order to harmonize your work with their concepts.
- Take simple, reasonable precautions including the use of disclosure, disclaimer and consent forms.

1.
LAWS AND THEIR PURPOSES

Just as one lives in a physical environment, so too one lives in a 'legal environment'. Just as it is helpful knowing about the physical environment, it is most helpful to know the basic structure and history of the American legal system.

Laws are rules of action. Good laws make for a peaceful, prosperous society. Poorly thought-out laws lead to moral, economic and social decline. As human consciousness has changed, so too have our laws evolved. However, basic legal principles such as the golden rule do not change.

The purpose of laws is to promote the unfoldment of the potential in each human being. To do this, laws should:
- protect the rights of individuals.
- protect the innocent from the guilty.
- provide equal treatment for all.

These qualities combined constitute justice and fairness. Often, however, laws are used to stifle innovation and competition in the marketplace, redistribute wealth, punish instead of making restitution, and manipulate or control others. The feeling of being out of control that everyone feels at times leads to the passage of multitudes of laws in a futile effort to impose control from outside. Whenever one considers passing a law, it is important to consider its actual and often unintended effects, even if its purpose seems noble and the effects are unintended.

Today, there is an attempt to create an entirely safe society. This has spawned an explosion of regulations and licenses in every field. In health care, education and other fields, many laws stifle innovation, protect outdated and often harmful practices, and protect the status quo. The actual effects of some of these the laws are the opposite of their stated goal.

There will never be an entirely safe society. Accidents will happen and innovation requires trial and error. This book will suggest that the best regulatory structure to protect people while allowing innovation is the free market. This requires strong property rights, full rights to litigate for damages, enforced laws against fraud, and a minimum of government-imposed regulations.

HISTORY OF THE LAW

For most of recorded history and in most nation-states, power and authority flowed from the gods to the leader, who then made the laws for his subjects. *'Might makes right'* was the rule. The Ten Commandments of the Hebrew bible represented a great step forward, as these were not arbitrary rules, but were for everyone and would be enforced by a power greater than any earthly leader.

Many of our present legal principles can be traced back to admonitions found in the Old Testament. An important lesson is given in 1 Samuel, verse 8. The Hebrews were told not to set up an earthly king or other idols. This follows from the Second Commandment. However, they insisted on having a king. Speaking through Samuel, Jehovah warned that a king would tax them dearly, take the young men to fight in foreign wars, and enslave the young women in his harem. The people insisted on having a king anyway - and the warnings proved correct.

Around the world, the 'divine right of kings' was the doctrine under which monarchs justified controlling the population. In England, landowners and nobles gradually gained power. This culminated in documents such as the Magna Charta, a precursor of the American Bill of Rights. Still, the king retained ultimate power. Christianity had a civilizing effect upon European law, but the church became a new power center that controlled through fear and dogma.

THE FLOW OF POWER IN AMERICA

The American Colonists, fed up with the petty tyranny of the English king and the Church of England, decided to abolish the position of king and to prohibit any state religion. The flow of sovereign power in America would be as follows:

- Ultimate authority or sovereignty flows from the Creator directly to each citizen (not to groups, not to majorities and not to bureaucrats).
- Citizens *delegate* (meaning assign or entrust) specific powers to the local, state and federal governments. This occurs by means of contracts called *constitutions*. These specify which powers are entrusted to the government and which are retained by the people. Governments may pass laws but they must conform to the contract or constitution.
- *All powers not specifically delegated to the government remain with the people.* (Remember this one!)

This was, and still is, a radical doctrine. It remains a shining light in the world. For millions around the world, it is only a dream. It has also been long forgotten by many judges, attorneys, teachers, presidents, bureaucrats and other public servants in America.

For the past 150 years or so, powerful forces have sought to reverse the flow of power, making the states and the people mere subdivisions of the federal government. This has caused much loss of individual liberty and social decay in America. *Liberty, privacy and the supremacy of the individual over the state are absolute values.* They cannot be bargained away or compromised without impairing the entire fabric of society. This truth is rarely taught in school, and we are living with the results.

THE HIERARCHY OF LAWS

Based on the above, there is a hierarchy of laws in America. This hierarchy becomes very important as one explores practice options. The hierarchy is as follows:

I. *Biblical principles* are the moral and spiritual basis for the American legal system.

II. The *English Common Law* embodied the biblical principles and was the unwritten legal tradition in 18th century Europe. America adopted the Common Law of England at the time of the American Revolution (1776).

III. *Constitutional law* consists of the contracts between the sovereign people of America and their federal, state and local governments.

IV. *Statutes or public laws* are laws passed by local, state and federal governments.

V. *Implementing regulations* are rules that accompany each public law in order to carry out the law.

VI. *Case law* consists of interpretations of the law made by judges and juries over the years. Important cases are called *precedents*.

Let us consider each kind of law in more detail.

BIBLICAL LAW

Biblical principles such as "Thou shall not kill," "Thou shall not lie", "Thou shall not steal" and "Thou shall not bear false witness" (which is fraud and perjury) remain the basis for American law. The bible traces the maturing of mankind from the slave state in Egypt to a state in which one is totally responsible for one's acts and thoughts. The Ten Commandments are the basic requirements for taking responsibility. The Hebrew word for commandment means a *signpost*, not a rule. The intent was that if one follows the signposts, one will be led to a better life. Other biblical laws include the 613 rules given in the books of Leviticus and Deuteronomy, and the golden rule in the New Testament.

COMMON LAW

Though rarely discussed, the Common Law is quite important. English Common Law was the major body of law in use at the time of the American Revolution. The US Internal Revenue Service law book contains a good definition the Common Law. Page 5041.1, Section 222.1 states:

> "(The) Common Law comprises the body of principles and rules of action relating to government and the security of persons and property which derive their authority solely from usages and customs or from judgments and decrees of courts recognizing, affirming, and enforcing such usages and customs."

The Uniform Commercial Code or UCC is a single federal statute containing some of the original common law pertaining to contracts. UCC 1-103.6 states that:

"The code (UCC) is complementary to the Common Law, which remains in force, except where displaced by the code."

The American Declaration of Independence and Constitution are Common Law documents. They were written within the framework of the Common Law, the system of law then in force in the American colonies. To understand the intent of these documents (and your rights to practice) requires understanding them within the context of the Common Law.

CONSTITUTIONAL LAW

A constitution is the contract established between the sovereign People and their creations, the state and federal governments. The word People is capitalized because it denotes a group of empowered citizens rather than a group of slave-like sheep. A constitution enumerates which powers and responsibilities are delegated to the government and which are retained by the People. Our state and federal constitutions also set forth the three branches of government and important details about the operation of the government. The federal Constitution is a relatively short and simple document that should be read and understood by everyone. Chapters 11 and 12 discuss the federal Constitution and Bill of Rights.

Constitutional law consists of our state and federal constitutions, including their amendments. Commentaries such as the Federalist Papers offer more insight about the intent of the federal Constitution. The first ten Amendments to the federal Constitution are called the *Bill of Rights*. All state constitutions also have a Bill of Rights. Many times the protections offered by the state constitutions are greater than those of the federal Constitution.

STATUTES

The state and federal constitutions permit local, state and federal legislatures to pass *public laws* or *statutes. Statutes must conform to the state and federal constitutions.* If not, they can be struck down as unconstitutional. Statutes have slowly replaced the common law in America. However, all state constitutions acknowledge the common law as binding unless superceded by statute. The U.S. Code or USC is a series of volumes of federal public laws or federal statutes. Each state also has its code book or book of laws.

Among the statutes are the *state medical practice acts.* These govern the practice of the healing arts and the issuance of licenses. An excerpt from the California Business and Professions Code, "Unlawful practice of medicine defined", reads as follows:

> "Any person who practices, or attempts to practice, or who advertises or holds himself or herself out as practicing, any system or mode of treating the sick or afflicted in this state, or who diagnoses, treats, operates for, or prescribes for any ailment, blemish, deformity, injury, or other physical or mental condition of any person, without having at the time of doing so a valid, unrevoked, or unsuspended certificate as provided in this chapter, or without being authorized to perform such act pursuant to a certificate obtained in accordance with some other provision of law, is guilty of a misdemeanor."

One may argue that medical practice acts violate the constitutional prohibition against passing laws that abridge the right to contract freely (Article I, section 10). However, courts upheld these laws under another doctrine called *the police powers of the state*. This is defined as the power to:

> "prescribe regulations to promote the health, peace, morals, education, and good order of the people, and to legislate so as to increase the industries of the State, develop its resources and add to its wealth and prosperity." - from Barbier v. Connolly, 113 U.S. 27, 31 (1885).

The extent to which the police powers may infringe upon constitutional rights to contract freely and protect one's property is an open question. The trend has favored giving up more and more rights and powers to the government.

There is another perspective regarding the constitutionality of the medical practice acts. Note that the acts begin with: "Any person who practices ..." A 'person', legally defined, includes corporations and partnerships. These entities are creations of the state. Such creations have no constitutional rights. If a medical practice act stated that "Any *citizen* who practices ...", it might be declared unconstitutional. We will return to this topic in chapter 3.

One can argue that the statists, or those who favor more government power, have tricked the population into thinking of themselves as mere "persons" (corporations), rather than remaining *sovereign citizens* whose rights cannot be taken from them.

IMPLEMENTING REGULATIONS

An *implementing regulation* must accompany each statute in order for the law to have effect. For example, a statute might establish a board of medical examiners. However, the legislature does not write all the rules and procedures to carry out the law. They delegate this task to an agency or even to the board itself.

Federal implementing regulations are found in a series of volumes called the Code of Federal Regulations, or CFR. Each state also has a book of state implementing regulations.

At times, a statute is fair but its implementation is not. Such corruption occurred, for example, with the National Labeling and Education Act of 1990. The intent of Congress was not to use the law to take nutritional supplements off the market. However, the American Food And Drug Administration (FDA) interpreted and perverted the law, writing the regulations in such a manner that they could remove products from the store shelves at whim.

CASE LAW AND PRECEDENTS

Statutes and implementing regulations are general in nature and cannot cover every case. When judges and juries consider specific cases, they further refine the meaning of the law. This is called *case law*.

Precedents are important cases decided by judges or juries. For example, the law says an unlicensed practitioner may not diagnose disease. However, when does an assessment, a guess or an evaluation become a diagnosis? This issue must be decided by a judge or a jury. All such specific cases form *case law*. Attorneys look to case law to see how an issue was handled in the past. Sometimes the intent of a law is just, but its interpretation by the courts changes its meaning entirely.

JURISDICTION

The next four sections introduce important legal doctrines that affect one's practice. The first is *jurisdiction*, a key to understanding our legal system and perhaps for defending one's actions. Jurisdiction of a court is *its right or authority to hear and try a case*. Jurisdiction also means *the sphere of authority or power of a governing body.* The issue of jurisdiction is the issue of whether or not a particular law applies to you, to your location and to your type of business.

Jurisdiction may depend upon a geographical area, the subject matter, or the person who is on trial. A simple example of geographical jurisdiction is that a court in a particular state has the authority to hear only cases that pertain to that state. Some states view natural health care differently than others. One state may be more lenient and therefore an easier place to work.

A very important principle of jurisdiction is that *in order to hear a case, a court must have jurisdiction over both the person and the subject matter.*

> "If any tribunal (court) finds absence of proof of jurisdiction over person and subject matter, the case must be dismissed." - Louisville RR v. Motley, 211 US 149, 29 S Ct. 42.

Another important aspect of jurisdiction is that once it has been challenged, it must be proven. If it is not challenged, jurisdiction is assumed to exist. Many people have lost their case in court because they challenged the *subject matter* of the case, when they should have challenged the *jurisdiction* of the court to hear the case at all.

For example, let us imagine one is charged with practicing medicine without a license. Let us also say that one does not consider oneself a 'person' under the law. The statutory laws are written for persons and the courts today are for persons. One would need to defend oneself by challenging the jurisdiction of the court. If one does not challenge jurisdiction, it is presumed that one accepts the court's jurisdiction and one can only argue the subject matter.

ENUMERATED POWERS

Enumerated powers means that governments may only exercise powers that are delegated to them by the People in the constitutions. All other powers are reserved to the People or the states. James Madison wrote in Federalist Paper #45:

> "The powers delegated by the proposed Constitution to the federal government are few and well-defined. Those which are to remain in the States are numerous and indefinite."

The Tenth Amendment to the United States Constitution states:

> "The powers not delegated to the United States (government) by the Constitution, nor prohibited by it to the states, are reserved to the states respectively or to the People."

An example of violation of the principle of enumerated powers was the attempt in 1993 to institute socialized medicine in the United States. The merits of it are one matter. The federal government, however, is nowhere empowered to take over the health care industry. A constitutional amendment is required to nationalize an entire industry.

Often laws are passed without the constitutional authority to do so. This abuse is widespread. The FDA often writes rules for herbs, vitamins, foods and other products, although they are not a legislative body. They have no constitutional authority to write laws. They also enforce their own laws, often with gun-toting SWAT teams, although they are not a court of law and they have no power to judge the law. Over 100 federal agencies do the same thing. This brings us to another important American legal principle.

SEPARATION OF POWERS

Another radical American legal doctrine is the *separation of powers*. In 18th century England, the king or queen *passed* the laws, *executed or carried out* the laws and *judged* who broke the laws. This gave the monarch absolute power. Every dictatorship combines these three powers.

To establish and preserve the liberty of the people, the founders of America decided to separate these powers. They asserted that no one person or group of persons would have the power to 1) pass, 2) execute and 3) judge the laws. They divided these functions as follows:

- The *legislative branch* of government enacts or passes the laws. Legislative bodies include local city councils, county governments, state legislatures and the two houses of the federal or national Congress.
- The *executive branch* of government carries out the laws. Executive bodies include city mayors, state governors, the president, the vice president and the cabinet.
- The *judicial branch* of government judges guilt or innocence. This is performed by the courts, by judges and by juries of one's peers, the People themselves.

Juries of one's peers were to be the ultimate judges of guilt or innocence. *However, the jury also has the power to judge the validity of the laws.* For example, one might be guilty of breaking a law. However, the law can also be declared null and void by the jury. Chapter 15 discusses this important subject in more detail.

This is a brief summary of how the American governmental system is supposed to operate. However, regulatory agencies such as the Food and Drug Administration, in fact, make their own rules, enforce their rules and judge who breaks them. This is a far cry from what the founders of America had in mind when they wrote the Declaration of Independence and the federal Constitution.

SEPARATION OF FUNCTIONS

A fourth legal concept I want to emphasize is the idea that certain government functions are best handled by the federal government, while others are best handled at the state level, and others at a local level. The distribution of government functions is a very important subject if we are to retain out liberties.

Declaring war, foreign trade, making treaties and valuing the money are *federal* government functions. Education and building roads are traditionally *state* functions. Police and fire protection are generally considered *local* functions. *In the 20th and 21ˢᵗ centuries, the American federal government has assumed more and more of the functions of state and local government*s. Some say this is the only way to assure a minimum standard for all Americans. Others say this is a grab for more government power.

The problems with centralized government include *micromanagement, unfunded mandates and big brother tactics that deprive individuals and localities of their rights and powers.* Others are *waste, fraud and abuse.* Any time another takes responsibility for our welfare, control and power are also taken away. Also, no constitutional authority exists for many of these functions. One might answer that times have changed and the old principles no longer apply. Perhaps, but perhaps not.

GOVERNMENTAL VERSUS PRIVATE FUNCTIONS

Another extremely important legal principle is that some societal functions are best handled by governmental bodies, while others are best taken care of by the private sector of society.

The founders of America reasoned, for example, that only those functions that individuals cannot handle by themselves such as declaring war, making treaties, building roads, regulating commerce, and a few others should be handled by the government. *Everything else*, such as building houses, repairing automobiles, manufacturing, retail sales, and industries such as health care, social welfare, and education are best taken care of by what is called the *private sector* or non-governmental sector of society.

The problems in American and European health care today, for example, I believe have resulted in large part from violation of the important principle of which functions are proper for the government to assume. I believe that the concept that a government bureaucrat, often with minimal knowledge of your needs, knows more about your health needs and is more qualified than you and your health care practitioner to make life and death decisions for you, is simply wrong. Yet this is exactly what modern statists believe and attempt to implement through legislation such as Obamacare, Medicare, Medicaid and similar "National Health Care" proposals in many nations of the world.

2.
LEGAL CONCEPTS ABOUT HEALTH AND HEALING

Now that I have explained basic legal concepts that should be taught in every Junior high school or middle school, let us move on and discuss how people understand heath care and its administration. This chapter concerns health care practices, but may be of interest as well to practitioners in other fields.

The current legal regulation of the healing arts is based upon an old, somewhat outdated paradigm of healing that I call *diagnosis, treatment and cure.* However, there exist several other ways to understand healing of the body and the mind. Let us examine this and other ways healing is understood and regulated.

The conventional paradigm is often called the disease entity model. One is either healthy or one has a disease. Health is thus defined in this model as the absence of disease entities in the body. When ill, one goes to a practitioner who *diagnoses, treats, prescribes for and hopefully cures* or gets rid of these entities called diseases. Those who diagnose, treat, prescribe, and cure disease entities are licensed allopathic doctors. *Allopathy* is a technical name for the medical system that uses drugs and surgery, mainly.

The above is the standard current paradigm of healing among most people, as well as legislators, judges, attorneys and other officials. It is very helpful and important to know this is the perspective of many people one will work with and among.

The medical regulatory laws that underlie and enforce this system are called in the USA the *state medical practice acts.* Each licensed group has their own law. The groups fight each other to decide who can do what to whom. This paradigm is useful, at times, and has served well in the development of surgery, trauma care and infectious disease care.

OTHER HEALING PARADIGMS

Other ways to understand healing are not new, but may seem to be so because they were shut out of the mainstream by AMA and drug company pressure years ago. They include:

1) Expand the 'diagnose, treat and cure' model.
2) The whole system approach to balance, normalize, harmonize and restore vital force and system integrity.
3) Detoxify the body.
4) Heal by intent, as in religious and spiritual healing.
5) Education, coaching and self-help.

These understandings of how to heal the body sometimes overlap, but there are differences. What is important for the purposes of this book is that each may have different legal consequences. Let us examine each one in more detail.

Expanding The 'Diagnose, Treat And Cure' Model. This may include:
1) *Diagnosing more diseases* such as chronic candida infection, hypoglycemia, yin deficiency, vitamin deficiencies, spinal subluxations and others not commonly recognized in medicine.
2) *Different diagnostic methods* such as oriental pulse diagnosis, hair mineral analysis, or applied kinesiology.
3) *Different treatment modalities* such as nutritional therapy, herbs, lifestyle change, homeopathy, acupuncture, manipulation and meditation, just to name a few. Holistic treatment does not exclude drugs and surgery, but these are generally reserved as a last resort.

Thinking in terms of this model of holistic care is commonplace, but definitely risky for unlicensed practitioners because it is so close to the medical model. Practitioners may be tempted to use words such as 'diagnosis' and 'treatment' that are reserved for licensed medical doctors.

The Whole Systems Approach. This is a definite departure from diagnosing and removing disease entities. *This is a process-oriented view of health and disease.* One's health is always changing in response to internal and external conditions. In this model, symptoms and disease entities are not primary. They are merely whole system responses to stress, imbalances and/or lowered vitality. To heal the body, one must honor the whole system and restore it to balance and harmony, rather than suppress symptoms and diseases.

This paradigm is both more ancient and a more modern system than the 18th century allopathic disease concept. The whole system approach today is based on general systems theory and cybernetics, which is a modern science of how complex, self-regulating systems operate.

Its principle is that symptoms are just a result of blocked or unbalanced vital force, or adaptive energy. Restoring health is a matter of restoring, balancing, harmonizing, normalizing, or promoting the free flow of vital force or energy. As this occurs, symptoms and disease entities go away on their own, without a need for remedies.

The wellness concept - that health is more than the absence of disease entities - is derived from this model of health care. Sciences that incorporate at least part of this model include nutritional balancing science (see *Nutritional Balancing And Hair Mineral Analysis* by this author), shamanism, chiropractic, oriental medicine, and others.

This model is more distant from the conventional medical model and therefore often safer, legally speaking. However, one must think about it and talk the language of balancing, normalizing and harmonizing the body to avoid legal difficulties. One must avoid regressing into the old allopathic model of diagnosing, treating, prescribing and curing disease entities.

Detoxify The Body. This model is ancient, postulating that toxic substances cause symptoms and diseases. Rather than fight diseases with more toxic substances, one detoxifies the body through diet, physical therapies, biochemical agents, electrical machines and other ways.

Toxins include heavy metals, chemicals, radiation, biological toxins such as germs, parasites and viruses, and metabolic waste products made within the body. To avoid legal difficulties, one must use the proper words and avoid speaking of 'diagnosing and treating' toxicity, which takes one back into the realm of the licensed medical doctor.

The detoxification model or paradigm is part of the whole systems healing concept, but also part of the old medical paradigm.

Religious Or Spiritual Healing. This model postulates that human beings are spiritual in nature and experience health conditions in order to develop themselves and learn lessons. One might even choose illness to avoid responsibility, to learn patience or compassion, to encourage oneself to grow wiser or to help another learn a lesson.

Practitioners of this model do not dwell on pathology or imbalances at all. It is a purely "down energy" system that is really etheric in nature. This means it concerns the basic stuff or energy of life. Some practitioners of this method offer counseling while others work with pure intent, sending thoughts of love or of "Thy will be done". These help a person to accept, understand

and appreciate the wholeness and perfection of whatever is taking place. Through this process healing can occur, such as in Christian Science.

In this model, illness is an indicator of our separation from Oneness or God. One may grow out of illness through increased awareness or, in the Judeo-Christian tradition, through grace and salvation.

This model is difficult to do properly. It is also safer legally because prayer, teaching and counseling do not involve standard medical tests, healing modalities or treatment systems. Problems can occur, however, if a counselor suggests that one avoid medical tests, medical drugs or visiting a doctor. Be careful about this, as it causes legal difficulty.

Self-help, Coaching And Education. Here the practitioner teaches another to handle his or her own health problems. There is little or no direct physical contact. Examples are diet and lifestyle counseling, movement therapies, yoga, tai chi, self-help massage and acupressure, and many other modalities. This model of care is generally the safest legally because the practitioner does not perform any procedures on another person.

LEGAL CONSEQUENCES

As a general rule, the further one is from the standard 'diagnose and treat' model, the fewer legal difficulties one will encounter. Expanding the medical model to include new diagnostic and treatment modalities is often considered practicing medicine, chiropractic or something else. Spiritual healing and self-help education are far less likely to be considered as practicing a healing art. However, it is important to observe the rules covered in the following chapters as certain words and actions are still reserved for licensed practitioners.

EXEMPTIONS FROM THE STATE MEDICAL PRACTICE ACTS

State medical practice acts contain exemptions for some aspects of the holistic model. For example, California has an exemption in their law for health food stores and nutrition counselors. However, one is strictly forbidden to diagnose, prescribe or treat any disease, mental or physical.

Native American healing is exempt in the Arizona law. Rolfers, Jin Shin Jyutsu practitioners and others have obtained their own exemption in various states. Ministers functioning in a religious capacity have an exemption in every state. More recently, Minnesota and California passed sweeping exemptions for many holistic therapists who operate unlicensed. This is a step forward. Here is an excerpt from Section 1 of the California law, Senate Bill 577, passed on September, 24, 2002:

(a) Based upon a comprehensive report by the National Institute of Medicine and other studies, including a study published by the New England Journal of Medicine, it is evident that millions of Californians, perhaps more than five million, are presently receiving a substantial volume of health care services from complementary and alternative health care practitioners. Those studies further indicate that individuals utilizing complementary and alternative health care services cut across a wide variety of age, ethnic, socioeconomic, and other demographic categories.

(b) Notwithstanding the widespread utilization of complementary and alternative medical services by Californians, the provision of many of these services may be in technical violation of the Medical Practice Act (Chapter 5 (commencing with Section 2000) of Division 2 of the Business and Professions Code). Complementary and alternative health care practitioners could therefore be subject to fines, penalties, and the restriction of their practice under the Medical Practice Act even though there is no demonstration that their practices are harmful to the public.

(c) The Legislature intends, by enactment of this act, to allow access by California residents to complementary and alternative health care practitioners who are not providing services that require medical training and credentials. The Legislature further finds that these non-medical complementary and alternative services do not pose a known risk to the health and safety of California residents, and that restricting access to those services due to technical violations of the Medical Practice Act is not warranted.

The act prohibits unlicensed practitioners from using medical methods, but at least legitimizes unlicensed practitioners and hopefully will avoid the fear of arrest simply for helping others regain their health by natural means.

Test cases will determine how these laws are interpreted. There remain grey areas of the law. If one sees an aura or places the hands on a person and describes how the tissues feel, is this diagnosing? I believe the answer is no. A diagnosis in medicine requires specific tests or procedures such as a biopsy for cancer. A natural healer who does not use the medical procedure may be guessing or asserting, but not diagnosing.

A judge or jury, however, may not agree. Do not guess or assert that someone has a disease unless one is a licensed doctor. If one believes a condition is present it is much wiser to refer to one who is licensed to rule out the condition.

A REGULATORY SYSTEM FOR THE NEW MILLENNIUM

Broad exemptions from licensing laws are simpler and less costly than having 40 licensing boards, as some states already have.

However, they do not solve the problem of incorporating holistic paradigms into mainstream health care. Licensing remains popular because it is a ticket to insurance reimbursement and participation in government programs like Medicare and Medicaid. These programs are paid for by everyone, but only reimburse for drugs, surgery and other mainly conventional therapies.

This book will suggest that a free market in health care services is a far better solution. A free market does not mean a free-for-all. It does means there would be no barriers or very few barriers to entry to the healing field. Current laws against fraud, misrepresentation, negligence and malpractice would continue to protect the consumer. Most important, consumers would decide the type of health care and which practitioners to patronize. Prices are set by what people are willing to pay.

America had a free-market health care system from 1776 to about 1910. The nation became the healthiest on earth. The passage of licensing laws between 1910 and 1920 destroyed the free market. America now ranks *last* in several health care statistics among developed nations and has some of the most restrictive and confused health care regulation in the world.

Today, modern conventional medical care is ruled and tightly controlled by a *cartel*. A cartel means a small group of individuals and organizations that control an industry for their own private power and profit. This is not the fault of capitalism. It is the fault of the licensing laws. These tyrannical laws keep the competition to allopathic medical care out of the mainstream of medical care. They also are used to limit the number of doctors, so that they remain scarce, are in high demand and thus costly, and it is a system that prevents real innovation because the licensing boards will not accept new methods of natural healing, for example.

3.
PRACTICE OPTIONS

Several practice options exist for the unlicensed practitioner. As you review this chapter, recall that *any practitioner, licensed or unlicensed, is subject to criminal laws against fraud or negligence if someone is harmed.* This is the reason the occupational licensing laws are not really the laws that protect the public, as is claimed. In fact, the opposite is often true because licensing shields medical doctors from prosecution in many cases. As long as licensed doctors follow "approved practice guidelines", they can get away with dangerous and stupid acts that would otherwise expose them to criminal prosecution.

Practice options for the unlicensed practitioner come under different legal umbrellas or systems. They either fall under the statutory, constitutional or common law.

Statutory options for working means those falling under the medical practice acts and other statutes or modern laws. *Constitutional options* means those that rely upon constitutional rights. *Common law options* refers to practice options that depend upon American laws that were adopted from the old British common law.

Here are the practice options for unlicensed practitioners.

Statutory Options:
1) One may work under the supervision of a licensed practitioner, usually under the same roof.
2) One may work alone or in a group, not under the supervision of a licensed person, claiming that one is not engaged in a regulated activity.

3) In California or Minnesota, or in any other state with similar laws that protect certain groups of unlicensed practitioners, one may work under a specific statutory exemption for unlicensed practitioners in your field.

4) One may form a private membership association, offering services to members of the group, but not to the public. This may exempt one from laws designed for the public.

Constitutional Options:
1) One may claim a constitutional right to earn a living, to help others protect their property (their bodies) by consulting you and the right to contract freely. Article I, Section X of the federal Constitution states, "No state shall ... pass any bill ... or law impairing the obligation of contracts ..."

2) Under the First Amendment to the US Constitution, one may claim a right to perform duties of a minister or a chaplin.

3) One may adhere to biblical principles and claim that one would be severely harmed by abiding by the statutes. The reason is that some of the statutes violate biblical

principles, and therefore would lead you to spiritual disaster.

4)   Under the Ninth Amendment, one may claim the right to offer services and the right of others to obtain services

Common Law Options:
1)   Statutes are written for "persons" under the law.   After studying how laws are designed, one may decide one is not a "person" in law. Therefore the statutes do not apply.

Which option one chooses depends on one's personal philosophy, the type of practice and knowledge of one's rights. The intent of this book is help you make an informed decision to bring the greatest joy and effectiveness while avoiding legal trouble. Let us consider the options in more detail.

WORKING WITH A LICENSED PRACTITIONER

The state medical practice acts allow this option within certain guidelines. This option involves close supervision. The licensed person usually must be present or must sign off on all work performed by the unlicensed person.   The licensed practitioner must be careful that he or she is not accused of allowing someone to practice without a license.

Many healers work in clinics operated by licensed physicians. Many paralegals work with licensed attorneys. This option offers a fair degree of legal protection without one having to learn much about one's rights.   However, one will have less autonomy and may earn less because the business is usually owned or controlled by the licensed person. Often this is only fair, since the licensed person is legally responsible for all that goes on.

One may gain some benefits of the statutes, such as receiving Medicare reimbursement and some limited liability. In return, one remains subject to most or all of the regulations governing licensed practitioners.

NOT REPRESENTING ONESELF AS A LICENSED, REGULATED PRACTITIONER

This option is popular, and is the option chosen by the author. One asserts that one is not engaged in a regulated activity such as medicine, psychology, law or naturopathic medicine.

Not representing oneself as a regulated practitioner often works well if one is careful and clear about what one says and does. The next chapter covers guidelines for behavior and speech to enable a practitioner to stay out of trouble.

One needs to avoid using the words, phrases, practices and even mannerisms associated with licensed persons. One needs to avoid actions reserved for licensed persons, such as drawing blood, giving injections and the like. This can be a very satisfying practice option. One may forfeit the benefits of licensing, such as government insurance reimbursement, but one is also not subject to all their rules.

As with any practice option, there may be legal challenges, especially if one develops a large practice, a visible practice, or if one threatens licensed practitioners in the community. In the author's experience, if one remains cautious and careful, cordial and focused on offering service, one will often not create serious difficulties for oneself.

OPERATING UNDER EXEMPTIONS FOR UNLICENSED PRACTITIONERS

As of the printing date of this book, California and Minnesota have adopted broad exemptions for various unlicensed practitioners. Other groups such as Rolfers and Native American healers in Arizona have specific exemptions in the state medical practice act. If one's healing art falls under such an exemption, it is an excellent way to practice. One should read the law so that all requirements are met. For example, the law may require a disclaimer statement, signing a code of ethics, or registering with the state. If your modality is not exempted already, one may lobby for an exemption to the medical practice act in one's state.

FORMING A PRIVATE MEMBERSHIP ORGANIZATION

This option requires establishing a private membership organization that all clients must join in order to receive one's services. Since one is no longer offering services to the public, perhaps one is not subject to laws designed to protect the public. If, for example, a licensing board attempts to stop one from practicing, the membership could sue the board for interfering with their private contract.

This option is interesting and used very effectively by some practitioners. It has been tested to some degree all the way up to the Supreme Court of the United States. It offers definite benefits and is not too difficult to accomplish. I recently did this and will report on its success in later editions of this book.

INVOKING OR CLAIMING CONSTITUTIONAL RIGHTS

One can try defending a practice by claiming a constitutional right to contract freely or to earn a living. However, experience indicates this *does not work* in court. As 'persons' under the law, Americans do not have full constitutional rights. One has only limited rights called civil rights, which are rights granted by the government.

MINISTRY PROGRAMS

Ministers and chaplains are permitted to offer counseling, teaching and non-invasive natural healing procedures including nutrition and lifestyle counseling, patient education, use of herbs and natural substances, and laying on of hands. The validity of ministry status has been upheld all the way to the Supreme Court of the United States. Ministers are protected by the First Amendment to the federal Constitution, which states:

> "Congress shall make no law respecting an establishment of religion or prohibiting the free exercise thereof, or abridging the freedom of speech or of the press, or the right of the people peaceably to assemble and to petition the Government for a redress of grievances."

Types of ministry programs. Most ministry programs are simple ordinations involving signing a few papers and paying a minimal fee. The case that was won at the Supreme Court was a "ministry mill" that just charged a fee and had no other qualifications.

Most ministry programs are offered by incorporated churches. These are churches that have received official non-profit status under section 501(c)(3) of the IRS code. Most churches are incorporated. Incorporating a church is a trade-off. The church receives government perks, such as the ability to issue tax receipts for charitable donations. In return, the church must file tax forms and report all its income and activities to the government.

Some ministry programs are offered by non-incorporated churches. A non-incorporated church does not seek permission from the US government to approve or disapprove any of its actions. It views its jurisdiction as outside of the government sphere of influence completely. An unincorporated church cannot receive tax-free donations.

Ministers versus chaplains. Some churches also offer a chaplain's program. This is a step beyond a ministry program. One must be a minister before becoming a chaplain. Chaplain status offers the ability to work freely in prisons and hospitals and to set up centers such as the Salvation Army operates around the world. It can also be used to set up natural healing clinics.

Limitations on ministers and chaplains. Ministers and chaplains are not permitted to perform medical procedures such as drawing blood, puncturing the skin or performing operations. One may touch another, as in laying on of hands. However, massage, for example, may not be covered. Any time a client undresses, a license is usually required.

Informing clients of ministry status. If one is a minister, it is best to inform clients of one's ministerial status. This can be done as part of a disclosure statement.

If one is a minister, does one need this book? One may ask, if I protect myself and my practice by becoming a minister, do I need any of the rest of the information in this book? The answer is yes. It is still wise to use disclaimer, disclosure and consent forms, and to follow the advice in the coming chapters about how to behave and think properly in order to have a professional and trouble-free practice.

A minister's certification is not a license to do as one pleases. One can still be sued or prosecuted for fraud, misrepresentation, malpractice, negligence and other offenses. The only protection ministry status confers is that one cannot be accused of practicing medicine without a license if one's activities are within the scope of a religious functionary.

ADHERING TO BIBLICAL PRINCIPLES

The Constitution and Supreme Court decisions have upheld a right to practice one's religion in America. One could argue that participating in the medical care system of the nation violates one's religious beliefs because some of its tenets and laws violate biblical principles. These might include abortion laws and others.

Therefore, one may argue that one should be allowed to practice a natural healing art because it is the only way that one can uphold one's religious and moral values.

This approach has not been tested in court to my knowledge. It requires a clear understanding of religious principles. I do not recommend it at this time.

NINTH AMENDMENT DEFENSE

The Ninth Amendment states:

"The enumeration, in the Constitution, of certain rights, shall not be construed to deny or disparage others retained by the people."

One may claim the right to offer services and a client may claim a right to receive services under the Ninth Amendment. One may says the medical practice acts can regulate licensed medical doctors or other licensed practitioners. However, if one is not practicing medicine with a license, one should not be subject to these laws.

Claiming rights under the Ninth Amendment has worked in some cases. Roe v. Wade, a woman's right to have an abortion, was a Ninth Amendment defense. This option is covered in more detail in Chapter 13.

The author consulted lawyers regarding constitutional approaches. No exact answers could be given as these have not been tested in court.

THE COMMON LAW DEFENSE - I AM NOT A 'PERSON'

An important fact is that words used in laws may be defined any way the lawmaking body wishes. All the statutes are written for 'persons'. For example, the California Medical Practice Act begins with the words "Any person who practices ...". The word 'person' in the law is a general term that includes people, but also includes corporations, partnerships, trusts and non-citizens.

Non-citizens have no constitutional rights. Corporations, partnerships and trusts also have no constitutional rights. They are creations of the government and totally subject to government regulation.

The American citizen should not be in the same class as these others. Yet they are all lumped together in the laws. It can be argued that the citizen is not a 'person' under the law, since a person includes corporate entities. The key question is, are you a *sovereign citizen* or just a *person* under the law?

The answer to this question requires a much deeper discussion of citizenship in America. Two types of citizenship exist in America, the original 'sovereign' citizenship and the Fourteenth Amendment 'subject' citizenship. This is covered in more detail in chapter 10. Also, refer to the resources at the end of the book for more information about this topic. While this is a very interesting subject, I do not recommend it as a defense of an unlicensed health care practice as it does not work in most cases.

4.

HOW THOUGHTS, WORDS AND DEEDS AFFECT LEGAL STATUS

Regardless of one's status and rights, one's thoughts, words and actions can help immensely to avoid legal trouble.

THOUGHTS AND INTENT

One's attitudes about life, healing, healers and other practitioners either help prevent or encourage legal problems. Also, if a legal difficulty arises, one's intent and attitudes can help one handle it with the least effort and complications. Here are attitudes that have served me well from a legal standpoint.

About Life Itself. Life is fragile, awesome and mysterious. In spite of studies and training, there is much I do not understand. Many systems and philosophies attempt to explain life, but life is beyond all these systems. Prudence, caution and respect for life are always in order. Cavalier attitudes about life have no place in any type of practice. If someone asks a question for which one has no answer, it is best to say "I do not know".

Motives For Working. If one's motive is simply to be helpful, educate, assist and facilitate others' well-being, one will avoid many legal difficulties. If money, prestige, power or control are important motives, legal difficulties are far more likely. *A Course in Miracles,* a spiritual psychology book, states that one's motive is either the extension of love or a projection of fear. Fear includes greed, anger, guilt and power over others.

Some become natural or alternative practitioners out of anger at 'the establishment'. This will often lead to trouble. Let go of grudges and judgments about other therapies or practitioners. If one does not like a therapy, don't practice it. However, it exists for reasons, which we may not understand. When it no longer serves the level of consciousness of patients, it will disappear on its own.

I entered the natural healing field due to illness in my family. I had no idea how much I was motivated by fear and anger at the medical authorities. It took a while to move through the feelings necessary in order to correct my motivation.

About Therapies, Techniques And Modalities Of Healing. Many systems and methods of healing serve different levels of consciousness. No single method is superior or appropriate for everyone. If one believes in only one way of doing things, one becomes a religious zealot. Legal and other problems are likely to result.

One person benefits from an herb, another from a chiropractic treatment, another from an antibiotic, another from a walk in the woods and still another from a religious experience. The client's belief system may determine which modality is most effective. Work in the way that is most comfortable, but acknowledge there are many other ways of doing things.

About Healers, Doctors And Therapists. Doctors, therapists, counselors and healers do not heal others. They facilitate, guide, inspire, instruct and offer help along the way. Healing comes from within, often from depths of consciousness of which we know little. A practitioner should feel privileged to be present when healing occurs. The healing power is in the one healed and nowhere else. Humility in this area is most helpful.

The opposite attitude, the arrogant idea that somehow one is responsible for another's healing, often lead to disputes.

Healing As A Journey. Healing is best seen as a path or journey all are taking, no matter their credentials, role or training status. The path of another is unknown. Refrain from judging any clients' or practitioners' qualities. Stick to one's work. Each has his place, even if one does not agree with another's methods and even if others bitterly oppose what one is doing.

If one encounters opposition, there is a lesson to be learned, rather than wallowing in self-pity, fear or resentment.

To avoid legal difficulties, *really listen* - to one's inner thoughts, to the clients or patients, to legal authorities and to those who would oppose one's work. Careful listening not only assists one in working with others. It also helps protect one legally.

WORDS TO AVOID

In the health care field, certain words have been assigned legal meaning in the state statutes. The state legislatures have declared that only certain licensed individuals can use these words. If anyone else uses them, they are considered to be practicing medicine, psychology or another regulated profession without a license.

Even if the statutes are not constitutional or if one works outside of them, it is very wise to avoid using words that are reserved for licensed practitioners. These words include: *cure, diagnose, prescribe, treat and possibly even the word disease.*

Instead of the word *cure*, use the words restore, help, alleviate, improve, correct, balance or normalize.

Instead of the word *diagnose*, one may assess, measure, check, determine or evaluate.

Instead of the word *prescribe*, one may recommend, suggest, advise, propose or offer options.

Instead of the word *treat*, one may handle, work with, relieve, balance, normalize, ameliorate, correct or remedy.

Instead of the word *disease*, use the words condition, problem, deficiency, excess or imbalance. Instead of naming diseases, use simple, descriptive terms. For example, one might say to a client, "I see you have swollen joints", rather than "I see you have arthritis". Arthritis is a medical diagnosis.

Words like 'naturopath', 'nutritionist' or 'psychologist' have legal meanings and may only to be used by licensed people in many areas. Regardless of the constitutionality of such laws, one needs to exercise care. Much safer words are consultant, coach, educator, or healer. Using the word 'therapist' is probably safe.

DO NOT MISREPRESENT YOURSELF OR YOUR WORK

Misrepresenting oneself or one's work is a fast way to create legal problems. Areas where this can arise include one's speech, stationery, business cards, website, handouts or other written or other material. Also, be sure to oversee the speech and manner of secretaries, receptionists, assistants or anyone else who represents the practitioner or the practice.

I once received a call from the Board of Medical Examiners when a friend wrote a promotion for a lecture I gave without first checking and misrepresented me as a licensed physician. Avoid even a hint of misrepresentation. Be clear in all communications and written material as to who one is and what one does.

Another method of avoiding problems is to avoid actually mentioning names when writing articles. In a rebuttal to an article in the Journal of the AMA, I mentioned the name of the article's author. This was completely proper, but he was deeply offended and threatened to sue me for ruining his name and reputation. He had no case as he was a public figure, but it cost me $1000.00 in legal fees to find this out. I learned it is best to debate ideas and avoid personal references.

At times, one can use a restricted word, say on a business card, if one clarifies the meaning. For example, let us say one has a B.S., Ph.D. or even an M.D. degree, but is not licensed. I was advised it would be legal to use the degree after one's name, but place an asterisk afterwards with a note at the bottom of the page or business card stating that one is not licensed in the state.

A friend was recently told by an employer she could not put her degree, Associate of Science, on a company business card. The reason given was that the degree alone does not explain the person's training and could be misleading. She needs to either state what field the degree is in, or leave it off her card.

An alternative and safe way to describe oneself is to list areas in which one works, such as nutrition, lifestyle counseling, health, personality or education. Do not use words such as law, medicine, chiropractic or psychology unless one is licensed in these professions. These are 'legally protected' words.

DO NOT DISPARAGE OTHER PRACTITIONERS

Speaking kindly of other practitioners is a professional gesture, but also very wise from a legal standpoint. If one has nothing nice to say, better to say nothing.

In particular, do not state that another practitioner is wrong. One never knows when one will insult another and cause the other to take action against one. Instead, say "I respectfully disagree", "I see things differently", "I have a different view" or "I am of a different opinion".

If asked about another practitioners' advice, avoid judgments like "that sounds crazy". Judgments end the communication. Instead, say something like "If I were in your shoes, I would not follow this suggestion". This leaves communication open and does not cause fear.

Disparaging other practitioners often confuses clients and can interfere with the trust a client has for you, as well as for others. In every field, many viewpoints exist. I have more respect for healers and other practitioners who respect the work of others, even when they do not agree with it.

Many clients are angry with their doctors, lawyers or other licensed professionals. They may encourage one to share or sympathize with their anger. Do not fall into this trap. I tell clients it is fine to feel anger, but then let it go. I realize the difficulty in staying neutral when one believes hurtful action has occurred. I am often called upon to undo mistakes of other practitioners. However, at times another may have to undo my mistake. Restraint is best.

Getting angry is a choice that can motivate a person to action. However, it is a choice that wastes energy and gives away one's power. It is possible to choose again. The essence of healing is taking back one's power and taking responsibility for all one's creations. In every moment one either spreads love or projects fear and anger.

This does not mean the client should not take whatever action is deemed best. It just means to do it from a neutral place, not a place of anger. Though I have listened to many horror stories, I have never recommended suing another practitioner. I respect everyone's right to sue, but am not convinced it is a wise idea. It uses up a tremendous amount of emotional energy and time, fosters the victim mentality and often keeps one sick. After all, if one becomes well it might negatively impact one's pending lawsuit.

I do not wish to be sued, so why wish it on another. I recommend an opposite approach. If one has not been treated well, be sure to thank the other and walk away. Better to focus on one's own life and work than on the faults of others.

STOPPING MEDICATION

By telling a client to stop prescribed medication, one could be held liable if negative consequences occur. Doctors often become furious with alternative practitioners who tell patients to stop necessary medication. Suddenly stopping steroids, insulin, blood pressure and heart drugs, anti-seizure medication and even anti-depressants can have lethal consequences.

If one does not like the client's medication, say, "In your position, I would probably stop this medication", or "please read this information about your drug and consider reducing it with your doctor's approval". One may also say, "our goal is to reduce your need for medication".

One may explain that medication can be reduced on one's own. However, it must be handled cautiously with full knowledge of all the possible consequences.

If one is very concerned about the effects of a medication, call the prescribing physician and politely voice your concern about his patient. Many physicians are not fully aware of the side effects of medication they prescribe.

SPEAKING WITH THE AUTHORITIES

Deal courteously with authorities. Be firm but polite. Give up anger toward them no matter what they do. If unsure how to answer their questions, tell them you will check and will call them back. Follow up on their requests and keep records in order. I have received calls from the state medical board, insurance companies and even an undercover police agent posing as a patient. *Responsible behavior is often all they are looking for.*

The undercover agent asked that I treat her father for cancer. I told her I did not treat any diseases, but I would recommend a diet and supplement program to help balance his body chemistry. I also told her about two excellent licensed medical doctors in town who offered cancer therapies. Both ended up in legal trouble thanks to her and both quit practicing rather than be harrassed. One did not fill out an insurance form quite correctly. The other did a cranio-sacral session on the woman, which she decided was outside his scope of practice.

ASSOCIATES

One can be guilty by association. If one discovers that an associate, office partner, employer or employee is not maintaining high ethical standards, act on it. If the person will not change, it is best to distance oneself from the person or situation.

To avoid surprises and facilitate problem resolution, put partnership and employment agreements in writing. This does not mean one is suspicious of the other party. The truth is quite the opposite. A written agreement is a sign of your respect and desire for a long and successful relationship. Include a clause that either party may end the relationship if one conducts business in an unprofessional manner.

Employees can be an important cause of legal problems. I had more legal difficulties with employees than with clients. Although I used employment contracts, was never rude and always gave proper notice, twice employees threatened legal action when I had to let them go.

Laws today often favor employees over employers. Also, one may spend more time with an employee at work than with a marriage partner at home. It is very important that employees' personality and qualities be compatible with yours. It is also easy to overlook these things when hiring if one wishes to focus on one's work, not on sifting through resumes and interviewing people for a job. Be sure to include in an employment contract that either party may give three weeks notice of termination for any reason.

TREAT PEOPLE KINDLY AND FAIRLY

A medical colleague has been sued twice because he is insensitive to his patients. Good service, and simple courtesy and consideration will avoid most problems. They also improve business and the image of one's profession. One always represents others in the same field to a public that may know little about what one does.

Unlicensed practitioners are often held to higher standards than those who are licensed. One can resent this fact or decide that high standards of ethics and conduct benefit everyone.

MAKING CLAIMS

A good rule is to avoid making any claims. Avoid saying "this treatment or product will fix your problem". Instead, say "it should help", "it can help", "it has helped others", "80% have been helped", "it is the best I know" or "I am hoping it will help".

Many get into legal trouble by making claims. Do not promise anything except that one will do one's best. Certainly never promise a cure! It is best to explain to clients that restoring health is an individual matter. There are many variables and approaches. There can be no guarantees in the healing arts. I tell clients I believe they can be well, but I do not know which method or how much effort it will require. If I cannot help them, I am happy to refer them to others who offer different approaches.

DO NOT DIAGNOSE AND DO NOT DISPARAGE DIAGNOSIS

Diagnostic labels have powerful effects. Do not use diagnostic terms loosely. It is awful to say, "I think you have cancer," or "I think your child is hyperkinetic." Instead, say, "I think you should rule out a tumor," or "you may wish to have your child tested."

Diagnosis is the realm of the medical doctor. A diagnosis requires a specific procedure or test in many cases. If one suspects a serious condition and is not trained or licensed to diagnose, refer the person to a practitioner qualified to make the diagnosis.

Some practitioners advise all clients to be under the care of a medical doctor at the same time they receive complementary therapies. This is not always necessary and can cause problems if the doctor insists on certain therapies. In general, do not live in a vacuum and try to handle everything oneself. Better to attempt a collaborative relationship with other healers and doctors.

MEDICAL TESTS

A friend who was ill consulted an acupuncturist. The friend wished to go for a blood test and the acupuncturist talked her out of it for two or three months. When my friend finally got the test, she was severely anemic and soon diagnosed with cancer. If my friend had been the litigious type, the acupuncturist would have been in trouble for advising against a simple test.

Always suggest patients go for medical tests if they wish, especially if not too invasive. Even if one does not believe in diagnosing, many people feel more comfortable with a diagnosis. Once the diagnosis has been established, one can discuss different approaches for correction. I purposely avoided the word 'treatment'.

PERFORMING PROCEDURES AND EXAMS

Rules vary in each state for performing various procedures. Drawing blood usually requires a blood technician certificate. One may be able to set up a laboratory account and refer clients to a local blood laboratory. Technically, one must be a licensed doctor to do this, but some laboratories are less than strict about enforcing this anti-consumer rule. Puncturing the skin and giving injections are often restricted activities, although one can give oneself an injection and puncture one's own skin.

Live blood cell analysis requires a laboratory license in some states. Having a client undress will cause legal problems unless one is a licensed practitioner. Using acupuncture needles is permitted in some states and restricted in others.

These days, even licensed doctors are running into problems with CLIA, the federal laboratory licensing bureau. If one wishes to perform medical tests, it is wise to check out the rules in one's state, especially before purchasing expensive equipment.

Laws governing the use of machines also vary, depending on the machine, how one plans to use it and where one works. Beware that many machines sold for assessment or healing are only FDA approved for experimental use, not for daily practice. This can create legal difficulties. When I have desired to use a controversial piece of equipment, I have not charged the client for its use. This may be helpful if a problem should arise. Assuming the machine is approved for regular use in a practice, some practitioners also use special disclosure and consent statements for performing procedures or using equipment, similar to consent forms used in hospitals.

DRESS AND DEMEANOR

Clients often consider superficial indicators such as dress, cleanliness of the practitioner and office, and mannerisms when evaluating practitioners. It is more true when clients do not exactly understand the work one does.

While one need not walk on eggshells, it makes no sense to make a poor impression or to dress or exhibit mannerisms that are inappropriate. One clinic director reprimanded a naturopath working at the clinic for walking around with a stethoscope around his neck. It may sound picky, but his point was that such a display is not appropriate for the naturopath, but rather is an imitation of the medical demeanor.

Dressing and acting naturally help reduce clients' fear and anxiety and assist the healing process. Comfortable clothing, and an odor-free and clean appearance and office are all that are required.

FEES VERSUS DONATIONS

A simple idea that reduces liability is to receive compensation by donation or honorarium, rather than charging fees. An honorarium is payment for a service for which custom forbids any price to be set. Healing and other services were often offered on a donation basis in the past.

One may have a suggested donation or honorarium. If, however, a person does not pay one will take no legal action. If one does not charge a fee for services, one may be less subject to regulatory laws. However, one is still responsible for one's actions.

The important ideas above, combined with disclaimer, disclosure and consent statements, will go a long way to provide a trouble-free practice.

5.
CONSENT, DISCLOSURE, DISCLAIMER, PRIVACY AND OTHER STATEMENTS

Consent, disclosure and disclaimer statements are wise legal preventive measures. Although one can screen clients and find out how they were referred, one never knows who is coming through the door. Also, clients may have misperceptions regarding who one is and what one does. Using a simple, clear form will:

- Improve communication between oneself and clients.
- Produce a better contract between oneself and clients.
- Help educate clients by clarifying what one does and does not do, and one's training or background.
- Protect against harm, both from clients and from authorities.

Some practitioners resist the use of legal forms in their practice. They feel it appears cold and unloving. I would suggest that a short, clear statement is just the opposite! The statement one uses should cover areas of consent, disclosure and disclaimer.

CONSENT OR REQUEST FOR SERVICES

This is a simple sentence clarifying what one offers. It can prevent a client from claiming he or she did not know what treatment plan or service was being suggested when he consulted you. The consent statement should be short and simple. It may begin with the words "I request". It might read:

> I request that Jane Smith do a nutritional evaluation and set up a program of diet, nutritional supplements and lifestyle changes for the purpose of reducing stress and enhancing my health.

> I request that John Doe counsel me once a week for the relief of stress and to enhance self-awareness.

> I request that Jane Jones prepare the following documents for me to assist me in setting up my corporation.

DISCLOSURE

A disclosure statement tells clients about oneself, such as degrees, courses taken, other training, experience or professional background. A short, simple statement is all that is needed. It might say:

> I understand that Mike Jones has a degree in psychology from Ohio University, an accredited school in the state of Ohio. I understand he has 5 years experience, 400 hours of training and has worked with about 600 clients.

I understand that Dave White has taken numerous seminars in estate planning and the preparation of estate documents.

Barbara Jones received her nutrition certification from World College, has ten years clinical experience and has taken classes with many leaders in the nutrition field.

DISCLAIMER

This is a simple statement of what one is *not* claiming or *not* intending to do. It lets clients know what and who one is not. It might read:

I understand that natural health care is not intended as diagnosis, prescription, treatment or cure for any disease, mental or physical, and is not a substitute for regular medical care.

I understand that the spiritual counseling provided by Jane Doe is not part of any recognized religion, nor is it intended as the practice of clinical psychology.

Biofeedback therapy can be most helpful to relieve stress but is not a recognized treatment for any disease or condition.

Robert Smith has a degree in naturopathy but is not licensed in the state of New Jersey.

Consent, disclosure and disclaimer statements can be combined into a single short paragraph. This is illustrated in Chapter 16, where sample forms are presented. The client should sign and date the bottom of the page containing these statements.

RECOMMENDATION DISCLAIMER

One may wish to use another disclaimer if one writes recommendations for clients. This one is placed at the bottom of any sheet of paper on which one recommends procedures or products such as herbs or vitamins. It might read:

> These recommendations are for the reduction of stress only. They are not intended as treatment or prescription for any disease, or as a substitute for regular medical care.
> (This statement does not require a signature.)

HIPPA NON-PARTICIPATION STATEMENT

If one is involved in insurance reimbursement or in a large office, one may have to comply with HIPPA regulations. HIPPA is supposed to protect the privacy of patient records. However, the fine print allows your records to be released to hundreds of government agencies and insurance companies without your knowledge. The government's real agenda, I believe, is precisely to gain easy access to people's private medical and other records.

I recommend that practitioners attempt to opt out of HIPPA. Ask about this and do not be bullied. If you opt out, you may wish to inform clients of this fact. A simple statement might read:

I have chosen to remain a non-covered entity under the Health Insurance Portability and Accountability Act of 1996 (HIPAA) that went into effect in October 2002. Participating would mean that hundreds of government agencies would have virtually unlimited access to your private records without your consent.

Your records will be released only with your consent. This office will not file electronic insurance claims. You may file your own claim and this office will provide you with any documentation you may need to do so.

NINTH AMENDMENT DECLARATION

This statement is covered in a separate chapter because it requires more explanation and background information for its use.

POLICIES AND PROCEDURE SHEET

Another very helpful document for one's practice is a 'Policies and Procedures' sheet. It is an informational form to save time explaining office policies to the clients, or as a redundancy to make sure clients understand the policies. It is an excellent way to avoid misunderstandings that occasionally lead to legal problems.

The sheet may contain a short description your practice, followed by headings regarding your policies. Depending on the type of practice, the headings may include:

- Treatments or sessions offered (types of treatment, duration and a short description).
- Initial visits (duration, short description).
- Follow-up visits.

- Phone hours or office hours and phone consultations.
- What to do in emergencies.
- Obtaining products and product mailing policies.
- Fees and payment policies (when payment is expected and if you take checks, VISA, etc.).
- Release of information.
- What to expect (reactions to sessions, etc.).
- Other, depending on the type of practice.

This sheet should be dated at the top, as fees and other information may change as the practice evolves. One may or may not insist the client sign the form. Designing a 'Policies and Procedures' sheet is an excellent exercise to help organize a practice. It also clarifies communication with clients and is for one's own clarification as well.

SIMPLER IS BETTER

I consulted several attorneys regarding the value of these statements and was told they help but do not guarantee avoiding legal difficulties. One is still subject to charges of fraud, negligence, practicing without a license and misrepresentation if one acts irresponsibly. These statements are valuable and helpful, especially if short, simple and easy to understand. The suggested form at the end of the book is intended to be as clear and concise as possible. It combines a disclaimer, disclosure and consent form, and a Ninth Amendment declaration.

6.
RECORDS, CORPORATE STATUS AND INSURANCE

Treating clients professionally and using disclosure, consent and disclaimer statements are excellent legal preventive medicine. Other important topics to minimize liability include managing records properly, the employee operations manual and other legal aspects of practice.

RECORD-KEEPING

Some practitioners are averse to keeping records. However, records may be very useful should a legal dispute arise. Licensed practitioners must keep certain records. Records can verify:

- When a client was seen.
- What kind of service or procedure was performed.
- The physical and emotional state of the client at the time of the visit.
- Comments made by the client and practitioner during the visit.
- Products, services or procedures that were recommended to the client.

Records to keep include:

Client Records:
- Sign-in, examination or interview notes.
- Test results.
- Treatment notes.
- Meeting notes.
- Notes from phone consultations.
- Copies of correspondence.
- Payment records.
- Other records or test results brought in by the client.

Employee Records: time sheets, checks or payment stubs

Tax Records: copies of sales, property, employment, business and income tax returns

It only takes a few seconds to write notes on a sheet of paper whenever a client is seen. It can be done while the client is present or just after the client leaves. Notes can be written or dictated into a tape recorder and transcribed later.

To save time, recommendations can be written with a carbon copy for the records or use a computer to store records. Record-keeping is also excellent to organize one's practice and keep track of business matters. Clear financial records in a computer, on ledger cards or some other system, are essential. Ideally, all records should be kept for five years.

Some holistic health practitioners fear confiscation of records and use of records against them in court. They prefer to keep no records or minimal records such as an appointment book. Evaluate whether this perspective is practical and wise for you. Paranoia or laziness are not good reasons to avoid keeping records. Some types of work do not require as many records as others.

CONFIDENTIALITY OF RECORDS

This is important. As a general rule, *all information shared with you by a client or in a client group is confidential.* You may not share it with friends, family or colleagues. This applies as well to test results, lab reports or other items pertaining to the client. To share records, you must obtain written permission from the client. Be careful with emails, phone calls and even faxes that may be seen by people who ought not read them.

Exceptions to the rule include if a client talks about harming himself or harming another. Also, records of minors may be shared with their parents or guardians. Records of disabled persons must be shared with one who presents a written power of attorney. Records may be demanded for a court case, but only by a subpoena signed by a judge.

There is a grey area and ethics is an evolving legal area. You may hear something that you feel strongly another should know. It could relate to an addiction, gun use, a life-threatening disease or something else. Use common sense! You could also consult a professional counselor to decide what to do. Note that you are not bound by a counselor's ethics unless you are a licensed counselor. You can download their Code of Ethics at **www.counseling.org**.

Larger offices must comply with HIPPA rules. These seem to protect patient privacy. However, the fine print allows insurance companies and government agencies unlimited access to patient records! Some offices allow clients not to sign the HIPPA form. See page 48 for more details about HIPPA.

THE EMPLOYEE OPERATIONS MANUAL

If you have employees, this is an excellent idea. It describes all the operations in your office and may include:
- What to say and how to address clients on the phone.

- Procedures for processing checks or VISA cards and making bank deposits.
- Turning on and off lights, heat and other utilities.
- Phone numbers for all sorts of problems with copiers, telephones, landlord, fire and police.
- Processing of tests, forms and client folders.
- Scheduling procedures.

While this is not directly for legal protection, it could prove useful. Let us say one's receptionist tells a client a particular condition can definitely be healed. The client is later disappointed and believes he was deceived by a fraudulent claim. It might be helpful to show that your Operations Manual specifically prohibits the receptionist from making claims. A mistake was made, not an intentional misrepresentation or claim.

INCORPORATION, PARTNERSHIPS AND TRUSTS

Some practitioners elect to set up corporations, partnerships, limited liability companies or trusts to operate their business. One becomes an employee. Benefits of incorporation include:

1) Limitation of some liability. For example, if an office is rented to a corporation and a person trips and falls in the office, generally speaking only the corporation is liable, not the practitioner. If an automobile driven by a secretary working for the corporation injures another person, the corporation may be sued, but it would be more difficult to collect from the practitioner.

However, one is still liable for advice given or services performed for others. If someone is harmed, most likely the practitioner and the corporation or partnership would be sued. If one gives bad advice, someone can still sue whether or not one is incorporated, a limited or general partner or working for a trust.

2) Flexibility and tax savings. There can be important tax advantages.

3) Separation of assets. It is possible to place assets in partnerships or trusts to isolate and protect them. One retains control of the assets. Having few or no assets in one's name can deter lawsuits.

Disadvantages of incorporation include initial costs, annual accounting and legal fees, extra complication and record-keeping. Corporations, partnerships and trusts are statutory entities, artificial creations of the government. In return for the privilege of operating one, one agrees to abide by whatever rules your state has regarding them. Discuss the merits of incorporation with a knowledgeable C.P.A., attorney or financial planner.

BUSINESS LICENSES AND SALES TAXES

Many cities and towns require all businesses to obtain a business license, sometimes called a transaction privilege license. It is a method of collecting more revenue and making life more complicated for business owners. If one sells products in a state or city with a sales tax, the business license may be combined with a sales tax license. Information about these is available from your city, state or county revenue departments.

A very important rule is *if one collects sales tax from customers, one must pay it to the state or locality.*

PROFESSIONAL AND OFFICE LIABILITY INSURANCE

Professional liability insurance, also called malpractice insurance, protects for mistakes in treatment. *It is never a substitute for high standards of conduct and ethical behavior.* If one is following good principles, one should not need it. Having insurance can increase the chances of a lawsuit, because a plaintiff may try to make a settlement with one's insurance company, as this is much cheaper than going to court.

Many unlicensed practitioners can obtain malpractice insurance. Practitioner organizations often offer it as a membership benefit. Unlicensed practitioners are often classified as "allied health professionals" for insurance purposes. The price is usually under several hundred dollars per year.

One company that offers it for many types of practices is Marsh Affinity Group Services, P.O. Box 5112, Carol Stream, IL 60197-5112, 1-800-621-3008, ext. 108. For practitioners of yoga, Reiki, reflexology, aromatherapy, movement, massage, kinesiology, fung shui and dance, the IMA Group offers professional liability insurance at www.imagroup.com or 541-350-0800.

Office liability insurance protects one if someone is injured in or around one's office. It may cover other situations as well, depending upon the policy. Many landlords require office liability insurance in order to rent office space. It is not expensive and is an excellent idea.

WORKER'S COMPENSATION AND UNEMPLOYMENT INSURANCE

Workman's Compensation is a program run by the state. It is designed to compensate workers who suffer injuries on the job or related to their job. It is a mandatory program for employers in most instances.

Federal unemployment insurance is a program of the federal government. It is also designed to protect employees. They can collect money if they lose their job, for instance. This program is mandatory also, and involves money that is taken out of employee's paychecks each month.

7.
DIFFERENCES BETWEEN LICENSING AND CERTIFICATION

This is the first of three chapters regarding the advantages and problems of occupational licensing. This is a current topic of debate among many practitioner groups. This short chapter carefully distinguishes licensing from certification or registration. The next chapter traces the history of licensing and the case against it. The chapter following concerns the psychology of licensing.

LICENSING

A license is a permission to do something that is otherwise forbidden. In most cases, a license is *required* or *mandatory* for engaging in that activity. For instance, a drivers license is considered mandatory to drive a car on public roads. Exceptions include nursing, in which one may be licensed or registered.

Licensing implies that the activity in question is a privilege, not a right. If the activity were a right, one would not require special permission to do it.

It is a government privilege or benefit. It may be bestowed by the federal, state or local government. In return for the benefit, the licensee subjects himself to the authority of the licensing board and many other rules and regulations. It is definitely a trade off in which one gains a benefit but pays by giving up some power and authority to the state.

A license involves the police power of the state. If one violates the licensing law, either by operating without a license or failing to uphold the rules governing the license privilege, one is subject to prosecution under civil or criminal laws. *The purpose of licensing, whether admitted or not, is control.*

TYPES OF LICENSING

Licenses are of two basic types. One kind are those such as driver's licenses and pilot's licenses. They are issued to anyone who passes minimal competence testing and other requirements. Their purpose is to protect everyone and assure minimum competence.

Occupational licenses are very different. They are privileges that allow one to work in a field. Often the number of licenses granted is restricted, and the requirements are complex and costly. Although supposedly used to protect the public, they are often used to control entry into and behavior within a profession. They are regularly used by cartels and special interest groups to limit competition and therefore raise the price their members can charge to the public.

CERTIFICATION

Certification is a statement or declaration that one has completed a course of study, passed an examination or otherwise met specified criteria. It is not a permission to act, but rather a statement of completion or qualification.

Certification is a private matter, issued by a private organization. It does not involve the police power of the state and is not a state privilege.

Certification implies one has a right to work. Certification provides the consumer with more information about a practitioner. Practitioners may use it to increase their competency through courses and to advertise or inform others of their completion of a course of study.

The purposes of certification are to set standards, educate practitioners and help the public decide which practitioners to patronize.

REGISTRATION

Registration is similar to certification. Dietitians, for example, are registered in most states. The registering organization, the American Dietetic Association, is a private group. The government is not involved. Information in this chapter regarding certification applies to registration as well.

IMPLICATIONS OF LICENSING VERSUS CERTIFICATION

Licensing presumes that an activity is forbidden until permitted through a license. Certification presumes a right to work. Chapter 9 explains this is a 'negative right'. This means that one is not automatically provided with a job but one cannot be denied the opportunity to seek work.

Licensing increases the power and scope of the government and decreases the power of the people to decide whom to consult for services. By the same degree to which it empowers the government, licensing decreases the power of the consumer and the freedom of the practitioner. Certification, in contrast, empowers consumers and practitioners.

Licensing restricts entry into a particular field of activity. Certification does not restrict entry at all. One may still practice without it. It merely informs and distinguishes those who have completed courses or examinations pertaining to a field of work.

Licensing strictly controls behavior. If licensees do not follow prescribed rules, they lose all ability to work. If one attempts to work without a license, one may go to jail. Certification controls behavior much less. If one who is certified acts irresponsibly, certification may be withdrawn. However, one may still practice the occupation, albeit without certification.

COMBINATIONS

Certain groups, including acupuncturists and dietitians have national certifying organizations. Some wish that state governments would pass laws stating that only those certified by the national group may practice in the state.

This amounts to a license. It restricts who can practice, it involves the police power of the state and it eliminates choices for the consumer. The national organization basically becomes the licensing board in a shared private/government agreement. The final outcome is the private certifying group loses power to the government. For if the government disapproves of the private group's actions, the government may repeal their privilege to practice.

Another type of combination occurs if one is licensed and certified in a specialty activity within the scope of a license.

SUMMARY

The definitions, features and implications of licensing and certification are summarized in the following chart for quick reference:

LICENSING	*CERTIFICATION*
A permission to perform an activity.	A statement of completion or meeting a standard.
Mandatory to perform the activity.	Voluntary.
Involves the police power of the government.	Does not involve the police power of the state.
Presumes that working is a privilege. Establishment of licensing shifts the activity from a right to a privilege.	Presumes that working is a right.
The privilege or benefit is given and may be withdrawn at any time by the issuing agency.	Certification may be withdrawn at any time by the private issuing agency. However, this does not stop one from working.
Increases the power of government, and reduces the power and freedom of consumers and practitioners.	Preserves and enhances the power of the individual consumer to decide the practitioner of his choice.
The purpose is to restrict entry and strictly control the profession or activity.	The purpose is mainly to inform and educate.

8.
THE CASE AGAINST MEDICAL LICENSING

Licensing practitioners to protect the public and hold practitioners accountable is often taken for granted. Having received medical training and practiced as an unlicensed physician for 32 years, I now see and appreciate another perspective. Nobel prize-winning economist Milton Friedman wrote:

> "... I am persuaded that licensure has reduced both the quantity and quality of medical practice...It has reduced the opportunities for people to become physicians, it has forced the public to pay more for less satisfactory service, and it has retarded technological development...I conclude that licensure should be eliminated as a requirement for the practice of medicine."(1)

Nobel Prize-winning economist George J. Stigler of the University of Chicago wrote:

> "As a rule, regulation is acquired by the industry and is designed and operated primarily for its benefit". (2)

Lori B. Andrews, Professor of Law and Norman and Edna Freehling Scholar, Chicago-Kent College of Law, wrote:

> "Licensing has served to channel the development of health care services by granting an exclusive privilege and high status to practitioners relying on a particular approach to health care, a disease-oriented intrusive approach rather than a preventive approach....By granting a monopoly to a particular approach to health care, the licensing laws may serve to assure an ineffective health care system."
> (3)

Ron Paul, MD, a practicing obstetrician and a Congressman from Texas, wrote:

> "Let us allow physicians, hospitals and schools to spring up where they are needed, abolish the restrictive licensure laws, and simply invoke the laws against fraud to insure honesty among all providers of health care...That will make health care affordable for everyone..." (4)

The idea of deregulating health practitioners may seem extreme. Let us examine why it is not as radical as it may sound.

HISTORY OF LICENSING

Many people take health care and other occupational licensing for granted. However, for her first 120 years, America had essentially a free market in health care services. Few licensing laws or other barriers to entry into the healing arts[1] existed. The American founders opposed licensing, a common practice in

England. They believed in 1) a right to work, 2) a right to freedom of choice for practitioners and consumers and 3) the government as a neutral party to protect those rights.

Herbalists, naturecure therapists, hydrotherapists, osteopaths, allopaths, homeopaths and eclectic practitioners offered services. Many types of healing schools and clinics operated without government interference or subsidies, which are rampant today.

At this time, America was among the healthiest nations. Competition between practitioners and healing modalities kept prices down. Low costs made health care widely accessible. The government kept hands off except that laws against fraud and negligence protected the consumer. No healing modality or group of healers had a legal advantage over the others.

Whoever helped people the most prospered. There was no need for insurance because health care was very inexpensive due to all the competition. Organizations similar to Consumers Union sprung up to inform people about the best doctors and the best methods of treatments. Certifying groups set standards for quality and training.

Many people used private practitioners. Others joined private associations such as the Lions Club or the Elks Lodge. The members paid annual dues and these societies hired doctors to care for the members and their families if they became ill or unable to work. Government welfare programs later drove most of these societies out of business by competing with them.

Others in early America formed *community health associations*. They were similar to HMOs, only much better because they were owned by their members. Their incentives were to offer the best care at the best prices. They were cooperatives that hired doctors to take care of their members. If members were unsatisfied with the doctors, they hired others. Laws giving tax breaks for employer-based health care did not exist, so if one did not like one's community health association, one could simply try another. A variety of church and community-supported private charities served those unable to pay for health care.

Serious efforts to change the situation began in 1847 with the formation of the American Medical Association or AMA. The AMA said they wanted to protect the public against 'quacks'. The real objective, however, was to increase the income of its members, the drug doctors or allopaths. A report submitted at the AMA convention in 1847 was unusually candid:

> "...The very large number of physicians in the United States has frequently been the subject of remark...No wonder that the merest pittance in the way of remuneration is scantily doled out even to the most industrious in our ranks ..."(5)

THE FLEXNER REPORT

The method adopted by the AMA to increase their members' incomes was to eliminate the competition by passing licensing laws. *Virtually every law restricting the practice of medicine in America has been enacted not on the crest of public demand, but due to intense pressure from the political representatives of physicians.*

The AMA's efforts culminated in 1910 when Abraham Flexner, a former school director and not a physician, was commissioned by the Carnegie Foundation For Education to evaluate medical schools. He was the brother of Simon Flexner, head of the Rockefeller Institute for Medical Research. Working closely with the AMA, he completed a survey of medical schools that was practically a carbon copy of a report the AMA had prepared several years before. The report found all but the allopathic or drug medicine schools to be "substandard". (6)

With plenty of financial backing, the Carnegie Foundation and AMA lobbied every state legislature in America to pass licensing laws to "improve health care". The government, they suggested, should also subsidize the new pharmaceutical industry and drug research. Their efforts succeeded, sadly, and by 1920 most states had licensing laws. The number of healing schools fell from 140 in 1900 to 77 in 1940 (8). Non-allopathic schools failed because their graduates could no longer practice. All schools that accepted women were closed, as were all but two that trained African Americans. Only the drug medicine schools remained, and the AMA-led cartel basically took over health care in America.

Licensing remains the basis for virtually total AMA union control of medical education, hospitals, clinics and laboratories. In recent years, chiropractors, physical therapists, psychologists, cosmetologists, naturopaths and others have pushed through their own laws in some or all states. Instead of getting rid of the system that shut them out for years, they have joined it, increasing its power and prestige. Many states now have 30 or more licensing boards.

THE QUALITY OF CARE

Any benefits of licensing must be weighed against the following problems of licensing:

1. **Licensing Restricts Healing.** Healing is a gift and an art. Many gifted individuals cannot, for various reasons, complete the 8 to 12 years of schooling necessary to obtain a medical license. Licensing deprives the population of the skills and art of these individuals, and prevents many gifted individuals from sharing their skills. The public is forced to patronize only those who can 'hack' the medical courses and exams, regardless of whether they are the most gifted healers.

2. Licensing Interferes With The Doctor-patient Relationship. A licensed physician is no longer responsible just to his patient. His loyalty is divided between satisfying his licensing board and satisfying the patient. The licensing board comes first if he wants to stay in practice. Anything that comes between doctor and patient tends to lower the quality of care.

3. Licensing Stifles Innovation, both in education and research. Not only do licensing requirements control what is taught in medical schools, but many government and university research positions require medical degrees and medical licenses. Yet innovations in every field often come from people in other fields who do not possess advanced degrees and licenses. Morbidity and mortality resulting from restriction of innovation due to licensing laws is incalculable. Dangerous older methods are used while alternatives receive little attention.

4. Licensing Protects Incompetence And Outdated, Dangerous Drugs And Procedures. Licensing laws protect "accepted practice" methods. These include many questionable and dangerous therapies and procedures. Many physicians are hesitant to deviate from the accepted methods for fear of losing their licenses. Also, it is harder to sue for malpractice when an accepted, but dangerous procedure goes wrong. Furthermore, doctors are much less likely to speak out and testify against other doctors, as they risk censure by their licensing board. Original AMA guidelines discouraged quality comparisons between doctors.

5. The Shield Of The License Results In Sloppier Practices. Licenses give doctors and hospitals an aura of respectability and often arrogance that results in mistakes and shoddy work. A recent article in the Journal of the AMA (9) revealed that medical mistakes are now the third leading cause of death in America.

EFFECTS ON COST AND ACCESS TO CARE

Licensing contributes to much higher health costs because:
- **Stifling innovation raises costs dramatically.**
- **Reduced competition among doctors and clinics increases the cost of services.**
- **Poorer quality of care and a sicker population raises health care costs.**
- **Increased litigation due to sloppiness and false expectations raise costs.** Litigation is an important cost factor in medicine today. Among other things, it causes physicians to practice *defensive medicine*. Many unnecessary tests and procedures are performed, all of which raise costs.
- **Complying with licensing requirements, many of which have little to do with patient care, greatly increases the cost of services. Hospitals in some states have to answer to 20 or more state and federal licensing agencies.**

Licensing decreases access to care because:
- **Fewer practitioners are available** and
- **Artificially-created practitioner shortages due to licensing inflate prices that limit access to care.**

OTHER PROBLEMS WITH LICENSING

If medical and economic reasons are not enough to question licensing, other problems with licensing include:

1. **Licensing Criminalizes The Population.** Medical practice acts convert thousands of citizens into criminals, although they have done no harm. In most states it is a criminal offense to "diagnose, prescribe, or treat anything, mental or physical, real or imaginary" (quoted from the Arizona Medical Practice Act). Heavy-handed tactics including raids by armed SWAT teams have been used to enforce licensing laws and terrorize innocent people.

2. **Control Tends To Be Tyrannical.** Licensing boards possess police power. However, their members are not elected by the public. Boards are mainly composed of members of the profession. Ordinary citizens have little or no representation, but must abide by decisions of the licensing board. This amounts to tyranny.

3. **Licensing Greatly Expands The Power Of The Government.** Licensing shifts responsibility and power from the consumer to government agencies. It is not a coincidence that all modern dictators have advocated government control of health care. It is an excellent way to subdue dissent in the population. If one does not go along with official doctrines, one may lose one's health care benefits or be imprisoned as mentally ill. Certification and registration, the alternatives to licensing, do not increase the power of the state.

4. **Licensing Debates Waste Legislators' Time.** An Arizona state legislator told the author the legislature spends up to 85% of its time resolving turf conflicts between licensed groups. The time could be far better spent.

5. **Licensing Increases Unemployment.** Licensing keeps many potential healers out of the job market.

6. **Licensing Severely Distorts The Health Care Marketplace.** Licensing amounts to a huge government subsidy of certain groups and healing arts, and the suppression of others. In other words, government bureaucrats pick the winners and the losers.

Such distortion has decidedly negative effects upon health, the economy and the quality of life in America.

7. **Licensing Creates False Expectations.** Licensing gives the consumer of health care a false sense of security in his physician that leads to false and often unfulfilled expectations. This contributes to dependency, and later to anger and frustration. The malpractice crisis is in part due to high expectations of the public, generated in part by the licensing of physicians.

8. **Licensing Is Discriminatory.** Licensing discriminates against the poor and the less academically inclined. They have difficulty meeting licensure requirements but may be superb healers. Licensing has also been used to prevent women, African Americans and other 'undesirables' from entering the healing professions.

9. **Licensing Creates A Privileged Class.** This was the original intent of licensing, but is accentuated in a modern welfare state. Welfare programs paid for by *all* citizens, such as Medicare, only reimburse licensed practitioners. In Arizona, registered dietitians fought hard to become licensed. There was no need except to receive insurance payments.

   Medical licenses also serve as 'tickets of entry' for thousands of government research jobs, grants and fellowships. Licensing is an integral part of a welfare system that redistributes wealth to certain privileged individuals and groups including licensed practitioners.

10. **Licensing Is Falsely Promoted.** Promoters of licensing claim it protects the public. Yet almost all pressure for licensing laws comes from the professions, not from the public. Existing criminal laws against fraud, negligence and misrepresentation already protect the consumer. These laws are far more stringent than the protection licensing affords. It is rare, for example, for a physician to lose his license unless he is convicted of a serious

criminal offense. Licensing boards do not like to punish their own members. Repeated malpractice claims, no matter their merit, rarely result in loss of licensure.

Licensing has made health care far more dangerous by protecting outdated and dangerous drugs and procedures, as evidenced by the industry's own statistics.

OTHER LEGAL CONSIDERATIONS

Medical licensing laws restrict trade and impair the right to contract. The U.S. Constitution, Article I, Section 10, states: "No state shall ... pass any ... law impairing the obligation of contracts." Such laws also interfere with an individuals' right to protect his property. What more personal and intimate property does one have than the body?

The Ninth Amendment to the Constitution states that "The enumeration in the Constitution, of certain rights, shall not be construed to deny or disparage others retained by the people." The right to offer and to seek health care services of one's choice was not guaranteed in the U.S. Constitution. However, this does not mean the right does not exist or was given away. This is discussed in more detail in chapter 11.

THE ALTERNATIVES

One alternative is to eliminate mandatory licensing. This would mean a return to principles that worked well in America for over 100 years. Without licensing, private certifying agencies would spring up to replace state medical boards. Many such groups already exist. One could still choose an AMA-approved, board-certified physician. However, one could also choose among a variety of alternative practitioners who are not presently permitted to practice.

Existing laws against fraud, negligence and misrepresentation would continue to protect the public. The public would be *better* protected from malpractice because no physician would be shielded by his license. Physicians would be directly accountable to their patients. Groups similar to Consumer's Union would spring up to rate practitioners, hospital costs and the effectiveness of treatments. A truly consumer-driven system would weed out the more dangerous and ineffective treatments and irresponsible practitioners far more effectively than licensing.

Health care would operate in a manner similar to car care. There would be many levels and types of care available. Not everyone enjoys the same level of car care, but most people receive care, innovations are permitted and competition keeps prices in check.

LIMITING LICENSING

In Oklahoma in 1994, the state legislature voted to restrict the power of the state medical board to regulating only allopathic doctors. This is quite a revolutionary idea. It means that one can practice healing without a license as long as one does not hold oneself out as a medical doctor. In all other states, the medical board regulates everyone except those with specific exemptions to the law.

Naturopathy. In the field of naturopathy, practitioners are split. One group, represented by the American Association of Naturopathic Physicians, desires licensing for all naturopaths. The other group, represented by the American Naturopathic Medical Association, opposes licensing. Similar splits also exist in other healing arts such as acupuncture and nutrition.

BROAD EXEMPTIONS

Minnesota and California have opened up the healing field somewhat by adding broad exemptions to their state medical practice acts. These permit some unlicensed practitioners to offer services without fearing arrest for practicing medicine without a license. However, the allopathic or drug medicine union remains firmly in control of hospitals, doctors, laboratories and other health care facilities.

REGISTRATION

Dietitians, nurses and others may be registered instead of licensed. All who meet qualifications are listed in a registry used to establish eligibility for employment. The threat of loss of registration polices the registered healers. The government is not involved. This is basically the same as certification.

Registration becomes like licensing if the government in any way favors registered practitioners or punishes unregistered practitioners.

CONCLUSION

It is easy for health practitioners to take advantage of the sick and debilitated. One is led to believe that licensing is the way to control this problem. However, licensing does a poor job of protecting the public. Existing criminal laws are much better for that purpose. Licensing was instituted to reduce the number and variety of health practitioners, increase the income of one group, and control physicians and the public alike.

Positive aspects of licensing are that it prevents some abuses and creates a more standardized, if lower quality of care. Also, for holistic practitioners, licensing may provide protection from the state Board of Medical Examiners. In Arizona, for example, the homeopathic, naturopathic, and chiropractic boards protect some holistic practitioners from the control of the medical board. The negative effects of licensing include lower quality of care, reduced access to care, greatly increased costs and much poorer health of the public. Its major drawback is the terrible loss of millions of opportunities for healing.

America did very well without health practitioner licensing for many years. As one looks for causes of the health care dilemmas the nation faces, licensing need to be considered. Perhaps it is time to join Milton Friedman and other prominent economists and question the blind belief in licensing.

Notes

1. From "Medical Licensure" by Milton Friedman, in The Dangers of Socialized Medicine, ed. by Hornberger and Ebeling, Future of Freedom Foundation, Fairfax, Va. 1994, p.68.

2. Andrews, Lori B., Deregulating Doctoring: Do Medical Licensing Laws Meet Today's Health Care Needs?, People's Medical Society, 1983, 1986.

3. Andrews, L., ibid. See also: The Shadow Health Care System: Regulation of Alternative Health Care Providers by Lori. B Andrews, Houston Law Review, Vol. 32, #5, 1996.

4. Ron Paul, MD, "Health Care", Health Freedom News, Monrovia, CA, February 1989, pp.18-19.

5. Goodman, J. and Musgrave, G., Patient Power, Cato Institute, 1992, p.140.

6. "Proceedings of the National Medical Convention", N.Y. Journal of Medicine, 9 (July 1847):115.

7. Abraham Flexner, Medical Education in the United States and Canada, Bulletin #4, Carnegie Foundation for the Advancement of Teaching, 1910.

8. U.S. Bureau of the Census, Historical Statistics of the United States, Colonial Times to 1970, Bicentennial Edition, Part 2, Series B 275-90, pp.75-76.

9. JAMA, 284; pp.483-485, July 26, 2000.

9.
THE PSYCHOLOGY OF LICENSING

If licensing does not work well, why is it so popular? In part, the public is brainwashed by clever public relations that favors licensing. However, psychological and emotional reasons for licensing may be more important.

AVOIDING RESPONSIBILITY

Licensing is a way practitioners avoid full responsibility to their clients. One who is licensed gains some legal protection as long as he or she 'just follows orders' given by the licensing board.

THE NEED FOR AUTHORITIES

Many people feel insecure inside and look to outside authorities to tell them they are safe and doing the right thing. Licensing boards fulfill this role. They may offer little substance, but provide a type of approval that many people crave.

For many children, an authoritarian upbringing stifles their ability to become secure, independent workers and decision makers. They remain dependent children inside. Distrusting one's own judgment also leads to distrusting others. Fearful of making decisions, one becomes fearful of allowing others to make decisions for themselves.

Such people feel they must have permission to work. They also believe licensing is essential to prevent fraud and chaos. The public cannot decide for themselves and they must be told by licensing authorities whom to patronize.

One who trusts and loves oneself has no reason to ask for permission from the government to be a healer, an educator or anything else. It makes little sense. A bureaucrat living hundreds of miles away is hardly in a position to judge the quality of one's work.

THE PSYCHOLOGY OF CONTROL

Licensing is really about control. It controls licensees, choices the public may make and anyone who attempts to work without a license. It controls innovation, education, prices and the flow of billions of dollars of research money.

Many people feel out of control and do not like the feeling. Instead of examining why that feeling exists, the need for control is projected outside oneself onto authorities such as the government. The appearance of outside control is a substitute for feeling in control within.

THE SAFE SOCIETY

Many people feel the world is unsafe. Safety is the basis for the promotion of licensing. It matters not that the claim is false and impossible to realize. It makes no difference that licensing offers a shield for bad medical practice and protects outdated and dangerous procedures. The perceived need for safety is so great in many people they will accept anything that promises it.

INCREASING POWER OVER OTHERS

Licensing often receives a boost from legislators. They know consciously or unconsciously that with each new licensing board, the government, meaning themselves, obtains more power. An activity over which they had no say is now within their sphere of influence.

Some legislators are simply power-hungry. Others believe they know what is best for everyone. Either way, too many are eager to take power and responsibility away from the people, always seemingly with the best of intentions.

Licensing also creates new constituencies for legislators. With the stroke of a pen, hundreds or thousands more citizens will donate money to candidates who promise to protect their licensing boards and special privileges.

Licensed schools can charge higher tuition fees, attract more research money and receive other perks as a result of licensing. They will fight hard to maintain licensing laws for all these reasons. Once started, licensing is thus hard to reverse.

SELF-PERPETUATION AMONG LICENSEES

Many who were shut out by licensing such as chiropractors and naturopaths, turn around and want to shut out others by the same method. Instead of dismantling the system that harmed their profession, they perpetuate and expand it.

If one is traumatized, a common response to minimize pain is to believe it really is not so bad and may even be good. This helps one tolerate the shock and is called the "Stockholm syndrome". It occurs in hostage situations when a hostage takes the side of his captors to deflect the horror he feels. One minimizes the pain by going along.

If one is forced to pay dearly for a license by years of schooling, for example, one may deflect one's pain by rationalizing that the license is a good thing.

A related attitude is "if I had to get the license, others should have to as well. It is not fair that others should not suffer as I have". This is a strange mentality, but one hears it often.

PRIDE AND EGO

Some practitioners, legislators and members of the public appreciate licenses as symbols of distinction, marks of official achievement, greatness and superiority. This resembles the way some students of karate display their colored belts as symbols of achievement for all to see.

CONCLUSION

The rationale for occupational licensing is largely an emotional one. Fear, distrust, self-hatred, ego and often a desire to avoid full responsibility explain much of the drive for licensing.

Understanding the emotional reasons for licensing helps one handle pressures to institute licensing and to respond correctly. One can realize it is not necessary to ask permission to work, and that giving one's power to external authorities is never helpful.

One can transcend one's upbringing and take full responsibility for one's actions. The next chapter shows this is what the founders had in mind for America.

10.
WHAT ARE YOUR RIGHTS?

A *right* is a power vested in a person by law. Several basic types of rights exist. This chapter discusses natural rights, civil rights, negative and positive rights, individual and group rights and privileges versus rights. Understanding rights in more depth can help evaluate practice options.

SOVEREIGNTY

Understanding rights begins with the principle of sovereignty. Sovereign means *superior in rank and reining over all*. 'The sovereign' was also a title used to describe kings and queens.

Until the American colonies broke away from England, they were ruled by the king of England. When they declared independence, they proclaimed a radical idea. They said *the people are sovereign*. The people are most important and reigning over all. So strong was the feeling of the sovereignty of the common man, that the American Constitution forbids the granting or use of titles of nobility in America. The United States Supreme Court stated:

"Under our system the people, who are there (in England) called subjects, are here the sovereign ..." - United States v. Lee, 106 U.S. 196 at 208.

The idea of sovereignty resting in the people is so radical that a book about the American Revolution was titled *The Five Thousand Year Leap*. No other large nation in history had proclaimed the people as sovereign before. Communism claimed to glorify the working class or proletariat, but it was the class that was glorified, *not each individual*. In fact, Communism just created a new privileged class, the party members.

Americans, despite ignorance of their national heritage and plenty of foreign policy blunders, are the envy of most people. This is one reason why dictators, whether in Communist Russia, Nazi Germany, Imperialist Japan or fundamentalist Iran or Iraq hated and will always hate America and what she stands for.

SHARED SOVEREIGNTY

Sovereignty of the people does not mean one may rob or kill another person, as the King of England did. Rather, Americans *share* sovereignty with their fellow citizens. *One's sovereignty is limited by the rights of others.* However, one does not share sovereignty with the government. The people are superior to the government, although one would scarcely know this by the way things operate today. The American federal Constitution states that the people have a right to alter or even abolish the government if it no longer serves their needs.

Millions of lives were given to protect the rights and sovereignty of the American people. While the principles have been forgotten and corrupted, as long as the Constitution exists they remain, waiting for Americans to rediscover them and to claim their rightful heritage.

NATURAL RIGHTS

The Declaration of Independence is concerned with *natural rights*. These are rights derived from The Creator, not offered by a king or government. This doctrine is essential as a basis for practicing trades without licenses. The Declaration of Independence states:

> "We hold these truths to be self-evident that all men are created equal, that they are endowed *by their Creator* with certain unalienable rights, that among these are life, liberty and the pursuit of happiness.."

This statement is based on the Virginia Bill of Rights. Article I states:

> "That all Men are by Nature equally free and independent, and have certain inherent Rights, of which, when they enter into a State of Society, they cannot, by any Compact, deprive or divest their Posterity; namely, the Enjoyment of Life and Liberty, with the Means of acquiring and possessing Property, and pursuing and obtaining Happiness and Safety."

In the Declaration of Independence the truths are *self-evident*. This means they are not open to question or the need for proof. The rights are also *unalienable*. Within this word is the word 'lien', which means an attachment or condition. Unalienable means no conditions can be placed upon them.

A theme of this book is that one does not go to the government asking for rights to practice one's trade. Government is not the source of rights, but exists to protect rights that come from the Creator.

CIVIL RIGHTS

Leaders today prefer the people remain ignorant about natural rights, because the leaders have no control over these. Instead, there is much talk about *civil rights*. *Civil rights are those bestowed by a government.* Unlike natural rights, civil rights can be changed or entirely taken away at the whim of lawmakers.

Some legal scholars claim the Fourteenth Amendment changed all our rights to civil rights and did away with natural rights. Perhaps, but I doubt it because the founders of America clearly based the entire American legal structure on natural rights. The concept had developed over centuries in England. Civil rights are fleeting and ephemeral, while natural rights are based on the dignity of each human being. The concept of 'human rights' is vague but related to the concept of natural rights.

The doctrine of natural rights is a check on governmental power. No wonder certain interests would not want natural rights emphasized in law school curricula and promoted among the people. The drift away from natural rights is part of the trend, particularly in the 20th century, toward greater governmental control in America.

NEGATIVE AND POSITIVE RIGHTS

The Constitution secures both *negative* and *positive rights*. This is an important distinction. *A positive right is an entitlement, promising a good or service. A negative right is a prohibition against interference.*

For example, the rights to freedom of speech and worship are negative rights. They prohibit anyone, including the government, from interfering with one's speech or worship. They do not mean the government must give each citizen a radio station or a church. These would be positive rights. Similarly, the right to own guns is a negative right. It is a prohibition against interfering with gun ownership. A positive right to gun ownership would mean the government must buy each citizen a gun.

Positive rights in the Constitution are rights to a trial by jury and the right to an attorney to represent oneself in any trial if one cannot afford one's own attorney. Here the citizens are promised specific goods or services. The distinction is very important because of the implications of each type of right.

Health care is a good example. Many people say there is 'right to health care'. First, there is no such thing in the Constitution, although the idea was discussed. However, there are two possible rights to consider. A *positive right to health care* means the government must provide health care. A *negative right* means no one can interfere with one's choice of health care.

Enormous differences exist between the two. The positive right creates difficult dilemmas. How much health care will each receive, when and what kind? Who will decide these issues and who will pay for it? Problems of positive rights include the following:

1) **Violation Of The Rights Of Others.** Someone must provide and pay for the promised goods and services. This quickly can become very costly as the government must pay all of the service providers. It also may place the government in competition with other service providers who for whatever reason are not hired by the government to provide the promised goods and services. In this way, for example, the US federal government has put out of business most of the private welfare societies and many charities that formerly took care of the poor and disabled in America.

2) **Huge Costs.** 'Free' health care, welfare and other entitlements are also very costly because there are no market controls. Waste, fraud and abuse are also costly. Costs of Medicare and Medicaid are already out of control.

3) **Distortion Of The Marketplace And Political Manipulation.** Positive rights or 'entitlements' such as Medicare and Medicaid are targets of constant political bickering regarding which providers and services will be included. Special interests and cartels have a field day with these programs. Decisions are removed from the consumer, grossly distorting the marketplace for services.

In contrast, a *negative right* to health care compels no one, does not raise taxes, does not politicize the issue and does not violate anyone's rights.

GROUP RIGHTS VERSUS INDIVIDUAL RIGHTS

Natural rights apply only to individuals. No one is superior in the eyes of the Creator. Today, however, many groups compete for special *group civil rights* such as minority rights, women's rights, gay rights and others. Affirmative action is based on special group rights. These are departures from the original concept of rights and often create anger and resentment. They divide people by superficial qualities such as where they were born, what their genital organs look like the color of their skin, or with whom they like to have sex.

The government's role in the American Constitution is to protect each person's rights. Group rights are based on a totally different view of the role of government. Group right are concerned with using laws and government to redistribute wealth or balance out differences among groups. This movement is called 'social justice'. This is related to 'political correctness' in which words or actions are deemed harmful whether or not they cause harm, simply because one *might* offend another.

Group rights cause many problems. Who should receive favors this year, what rights or privileges should be given, what about those hurt in the process, and on what basis will these decisions be made? Group rights create a politics of class envy, race envy, and more. The legislature is the place one goes for special favors rather than protecting all the people's rights.

Using laws to make up for past abuses is unjust to innocent people living now. Reverse discrimination is still discrimination. Opposing special rights does not mean one opposes women, gays or others.

It is demeaning to classify people by their race, skin color or sex. Group rights laws do exactly that. Laws should minimize differences, not accentuate them. Blaming all white people for the abuses of a few dead ancestors is simple racism. Lumping all white people together is as distorted and incorrect as any other prejudice. I would suggest that even classifying people by income has no place under the principles of American justice. It is simply no one else's business.

One may answer that slavery and women's rights were ignored when the country began. This is true and these shortcomings, products of the time period, have been remedied. Why start a new round of prejudice?

Today, affirmative action and other group rights are beginning to be questioned. Many realize that favoring one group over another for any reason produces anger and divisiveness. If the law is to prevent discrimination, it must treat everyone equally. The law is not for social engineering. Using it to redistribute wealth has not worked well. Let us hope we abandon this very un-American idea.

RIGHTS VERSUS PRIVILEGES

People often confuse rights with privileges. A license, for example, does not confer a right to practice a healing art, but rather a privilege. *A privilege is an immunity granted as a particular advantage or favor, or permission to do something otherwise prohibited.*

Rights are the same for all, while privileges offer special advantages for a few. Rights are presumed to exist although one may need to claim them. Privileges must be granted. Rights empower the people. The granting of privileges increases the power of the authorities, which tends to disempower individuals.

Rights presume that power rests in the individual. Privileges presume that power rests in authorities who bestow favors on certain people or groups. Privileges generally require a license or permit. It can be revoked if certain conditions are not met.

Natural rights cannot be taken away. Civil rights cannot be taken away except by an act of the legislature. Privileges, however, are often conferred and revoked by a variety of non-elected administrative bodies such as licensing boards, building departments and many others.

A trend in America is to change what were formerly rights into privileges. For example, occupational licenses turn the right to earn a living into a privilege.

DOES HAVING RIGHTS MEAN ONE CAN DO WHAT ONE WANTS?

Having rights implies and requires responsible action.
For example, since sovereignty is shared, one may be sanctioned if one violates the rights of others. Freedom for oneself implies and requires that one accords others the same freedom. Rights are also

be taken away if one breaks the law. The convicted criminal loses his right to move about freely because he does not act responsibly.

CLAIMING RIGHTS

An important principle is that *rights must be claimed.* They exist as potentials only, unless and until they are claimed. In court and even in routine encounters with police and other authorities, if rights are not claimed they are automatically waived. This fact may be important in some situations. It is stated as follows in the Uniform Commercial Code (UCC 1-207.9):

> "When a waivable right or claim is involved, the failure to make a reservation thereof, causes a loss of the right, and bars its assertion at a later date."

How to claim one's constitutional rights is explained in UCC 1-207.4: Sufficiency of the Reservation:

> "Any expression indicating an intention to reserve rights, is sufficient, such as 'without prejudice'."

'Without prejudice' means one does not waive any of one's rights. One may also say or write "all rights reserved". In an encounter with a legal authority, it is a good idea to state clearly that one reserves all one's rights. The Ninth Amendment declaration to be discussed in chapter 11 follows this line of reasoning. This declaration states that one reserves the right to offer services under the Ninth Amendment to the Constitution. Reserving one's rights does not mean a judge will necessarily agree. However, the principle of claiming rights is an important one.

CITIZENSHIP AND RIGHTS

Two American citizenships exist. The original *state citizenship* is defined in the Declaration of Independence and Article II of the federal Constitution. It is the sovereign citizenship, with full natural and constitutional rights.

The second citizenship arose after the Civil War. Instead of giving the freed slaves full state citizenship, they were granted an inferior *federal or U.S. citizenship.* It is defined in the Fourteenth Amendment:

> "All *persons* born or naturalized in the United States *and subject to the jurisdiction thereof* are citizens of the United States and of the state wherein they reside" (italics are mine).

This was the first federal constitutional Amendment in which the word 'person' appears. A 'person' in the legal sense usually means a corporate entity such as a corporation or trust. Notice the words 'subject to' which is the opposite of sovereign. *The freed slaves were made corporate subjects of the federal United States.*

Not only were the freed slaves not accorded the same citizenship as other Americans, all Americans are today assumed to be federal 'subjects' rather than sovereign citizens. All of the laws are written for *persons*, not sovereigns. They have to be, as many of the laws including the medical practice acts would not be constitutional if applied to sovereign citizens who have full natural and constitutional rights. The Supreme Court expressed the idea as follows:

"Since in common usage, the term person does not include the sovereign, statutes not employing the phrase are ordinarily construed to exclude it."
- United States v. Fox, 94 U.S. 315

This is a complex subject beyond the scope of this book. Most attorneys are not even aware of dual citizenship. Here it suffices to say that one is presumed by the government to be a second-class, 'subject' citizen unless one claims sovereign citizenship. Only the sovereign citizen has full rights. The 'subject' citizen has only civil rights, which are very inferior.

Many Americans are frustrated trying to reconcile concepts of liberty learned in school with the thousands of laws and taxes that could never be imposed on free people. Many become cynical as a result. Dual citizenship is key to understanding this issue.

REAWAKENING TO SOVEREIGNTY

The founders of America understood and articulated the radical political idea of the *sovereignty of the individual*. This reflects a great spiritual truth as well, that the Creator talks to individuals, not to government bureaucrats only.

This does not mean that one should never delegate one's sovereignty or power to leaders, as leaders are still required today. As a sovereign, one has the right to give one's power and liberty away. Most Americans have done so to a large degree, both politically and often personally. However, the idea of personal sovereignty remains in the founding documents of America, hopefully to be rediscovered by the mass of the people some day.

One may practice one's healing art, for example, under the illusion that one is a 'subject' - subject to the government and to one's fears, doubts and illusions. One may also choose again, acknowledging one's personal and political power and sovereignty, learning about rights, claiming them and helping others do the same.

11.
THE UNITED STATES CONSTITUTION

This chapter and the one following help one appreciate how much the founders of America desired to protect innovation and individual effort. They were familiar with the guild system of England. It functioned much like the current AMA and other trade unions that control entire professions to keep outsiders from gaining entrance. The material in this chapter is hardly taught any more, even though it revolutionized the world.

WHAT IS THE PURPOSE OF GOVERNMENT?

If natural rights do not derive from the government, what is the reason for government? The Declaration of Independence answers this question:

> "... to *secure* these rights, governments are instituted among men, deriving their just powers from the consent of the governed."

The concept is that government exists to *protect* and *secure* our God-given rights. This was a unique idea that is still not understood by most attorneys and lawmakers today. It means that the main role of government is a negative one. That is, it is there to stop others from infringing on your rights. It is not there to provide welfare for certain groups, to tell everyone what to do, or to set national policies, except perhaps in a general way and in terms of making treaties and conducting wars, for example.

Government is certainly not performing its task when it takes rights away, such as taking away the right to work unless one obtains an occupational license.

The opposite of this doctrine is called *socialism* or *communism*. These doctrines presume that government knows best and the rights of the individual must be sacrificed to "the collective good". This was the basis of the Soviet Union and is more accepted in Europe.

The American founders broke away from the socialist idea in asserting the spiritual concept that government exists to protect and further the potential of *each individual*. In spite of its failure, socialist thought is common in America, especially in academic circles and in the Democratic Party these days.

A CONSTITUTIONAL REPUBLIC

The federal Constitution is a contract between the people and their created entity, the federal government. The form of government it created is a *constitutional republic with democratically elected leaders*. A republic is rule by law. It is the middle ground between two extremes.

One extreme is a monarchy or dictatorship. This means rule by one individual or perhaps a small group of people. This was the system in England at the time of the American Revolution, and is still the governmental system in most nations of the world.

The other extreme, believe it or not, is a pure democracy. Democracy means rule by the majority. *Individuals and minorities are ignored in a pure democracy.* In a pure democracy, if 51% of the people vote for something, it becomes the law. For example, if

51% of the people do not like someone, they could vote to kill this person. Natural healers and other innovators tend to be in the minority, so this is an important issue to consider.

Only a true constitutional republic respects the rights of individuals and minorities. It does this with a constitution that guarantees certain rights and liberties of all of the people, regardless of their race, color, occupation or anything else – as long as they follow the laws of the land. This very important legal concept is hardly taught in school. Even worse, our leaders repeatedly misspeak when they refer to America and even European nations as democracies, when they are not. They are constitutional republics.

America was set up as a constitutional republic with democratically elected leaders. She has degenerated into more of a democracy because she no longer strictly follows her federal and state constitutions. As a result, majorities infringe on the rights of individuals ever more. This trend needs to be reversed.

James Madison and Thomas Jefferson knew well the problems of democracies. They watched democracy degenerate into mob rule in the French Revolution. Madison wrote that *the most dangerous centers of power are not the legislature, but powerful majorities.*

I feel it is no accident that our leaders refer to America as a democracy. Using the correct term would force them to adhere more closely to the Constitution, which limits their power and influence. America was intended to be ruled by laws, not by the whim of politicians or majorities.

POWERS DELEGATED TO THE FEDERAL GOVERNMENT

Chapter 1 described the doctrine of delegated powers. In the Constitution, the People assigned or delegated certain *specific, limited* powers to the federal government. Article I, Section 8 lists many of these. They include the powers to:

1) declare war;
2) make treaties;
3) set up two houses of congress to make laws;
4) set up courts to judge cases;
5) establish a 10 square mile area for the seat of government, to be called the District of Columbia;
6) establish docks, shipyards "and other needful buildings" within the states to conduct government business;
7) levy duties and excise taxes to pay for government;
8) levy direct taxes, provided they are apportioned equally among all the people. A head tax is such a tax. Income tax is a direct tax, but it is not apportioned;
9) coin money and regulate the value thereof;
10) fix the standard of weights and measures;
11) regulate commerce with foreign nations and among the states;
12) pay the bills for the nation;
13) establish uniform rules of naturalization and bankruptcy;
14) provide punishment for counterfeiters;
15) establish post offices and post roads;
16) promote science and invention by setting up exclusive rights for inventors and authors (patents and copyrights);
17) raise armies, but only for a period of two years;
18) provide and maintain a navy and to make rules to govern the army and navy;
19) provide for calling forth the state militias to suppress rebellions and insurrections;
20) provide for organizing, arming and disciplining the militia;
21) exercise exclusive legislation over the District of Columbia, the territories and possessions, and over forts, docks,

magazines, arsenals and other government buildings within the states;

22) enact all laws to carry out the foregoing.

Notice what is _not_ included. No mention is made of health care, welfare, education, food stamps or income tax (only indirect taxes such as import taxes were allowed). The founders did not forget these items. Instead, they felt these activities would be handled best by the private sector or the states.

The founders studied the history of governments extensively. They knew that government is basically force and that it handles some functions better than others. They knew well the tendency for abuse and corruption by bureaucracies and elected officials. _As a result, they opted for a limited government of specifically delegated powers._ Sadly, the wisdom of a limited government is being ignored by nations around the world.

In spite of the American founders' intentions, the federal government has grown enormous. Many powers have been vastly expanded or altered. Here are just a few examples:

* The Federal Reserve Debacle. The Constitution states, Congress _shall_ have the power to coin money and regulate the value thereof. The word 'shall' indicates this power may not be delegated. However, in 1913, the Federal Reserve Corporation, a private company owned by several families, took complete control of American finances. They claimed this would prevent recessions and depressions. Sixteen years later, America had the worst depression in her history.

The Federal Reserve Corporation buys paper money from the Treasury for the cost of printing and lends it back to the US Government at face value, with interest! The full story is described in _The Creature From Jeykll Island_ by G. Edward

Griffin. If I taught economics, this book would be first on the list of required reading.

As if this were not bad enough, Franklin Roosevelt and later presidents flagrantly violated the Constitution by taking the nation off the gold standard, beginning in 1933. Lyndon Johnson withdrew silver backing of the dollar in 1964. This left us with paper money with no hard currency backing at all. The government then reduced the value of our money by inflating it - printing as much of it as they wish. A dollar today is worth about 2 cents compared to a 1900 gold-backed dollar. Money is like blood in the body. It is the medium of exchange. The effect of inflation is similar to watering down the blood in the body. The hardship and suffering caused by private control and manipulation of our money are incalculable.

* **The IRS and FDA Debacles.** The Congress has two jobs. The first is to exercise *limited authority over the 50 states.* The second is to exercise virtually *unlimited authority over the territories and possessions of the United States and the District of Columbia.* These two jobs have become completely confused. Congress regularly passes laws that only apply to the territories and possessions, but they are imposed on the citizens of the fifty states.

For example, I know this sounds amazing, but the US Internal Revenue Service may only collect money from the territories, possessions and the District of Columbia. If this sounds unbelievable, check the IRS code, Section 3121 (e), which defines State and United States. Note that the 50 states are not included!

> **(1) State:** the term "State" includes the District of Columbia, the Commonwealth of Puerto Rico, the Virgin Islands, Guam and American Samoa.

(2) United States: the term "United States" when used in a geographical sense includes the Commonwealth of Puerto Rico, the Virgin Islands, Guam and American Samoa.

One might think that the word 'state' automatically includes the 50 states. However, this is not the legal definition of the word 'includes'. To prove this, in another section of the IRS code, Section 6103(b)(5)(a), they temporarily expand the definition of state and say it means "any of the 50 states ..."

The IRS technically may not collect taxes within the 50 states except from government employees working within the states. Similarly, the FDA only has jurisdiction over imported products. However, this limited authority has been extended by confusing the two jobs or jurisdictions of the Congress. As a result, these regulatory agencies have vast powers they should not have. For more information on this interesting topic, refer to the resources at the end of the book.

CONCLUSION

Many people today believe that a modern society requires a powerful central government. They have no use for the principles of liberty upon which the American nation, and some others, were founded. Deceit, mixed with gross ignorance and apathy of the people have perverted the principles of the American Constitution. Instead of the rule of law, today one is often subject to rule by the whim of judges and politicians. One can definitely trace social, moral and economic decline of the United States to the enactment of laws that pervert and negate the intent of the Constitution.

12.
THE AMERICAN BILL OF RIGHTS

The first ten Amendments to the American federal Constitution are called the Bill of Rights. The Ninth Amendment is a means to protect one's practice. However, the entire Bill of Rights is so important that its history and contents merit at least a short discussion.

A debate took place whether or not to include the Bill of Rights in the Constitution at all. Those opposed said the Bill of Rights was totally unnecessary. This was absolutely true. The American Bill of Rights is simply a restatement of certain rights that were presumed retained by the people. *Technically, there was no need for the Bill of Rights.*

The Constitution enumerates the powers delegated to the government. *All other rights and powers were reserved to the people or the states.* Thus, why bother *restating* some of these rights?

Those in favor of a Bill of Rights included Thomas Jefferson and James Madison. They already had a Bill of Rights in their Virginia State Constitution. They argued that it is the nature of government to grow, usurp power and exercise tyranny over the people. Therefore, some of the most important rights of the people should be stated in more detail. This would help avoid the tendency of government to take more and more power.

In spite of their concerns, the US federal Constitution was approved without a Bill of Rights. Virginia and New York refused to ratify it unless the first 10 Amendments were included.

Time has shown the wisdom of the Bill of Rights. America would be much worse off without it. Most people have no idea the intent of the Constitution was to reserve *all* rights and powers to the people or the states, unless specifically delegated to the federal government. I hope someday this truth is taught in elementary school, let alone in law school.

THE FIRST TEN AMENDMENTS

Very briefly, the first ten Amendments or Bill of Rights provide for:

1) The right to freedom of worship, freedom of speech, a free press, the right to assembly peacefully, and the right to petition the government for redress of grievances.

2) The right to own and carry weapons without interference.

3) The right to consent if a government wants to quarter troops in one's home.

4) The right to be secure in one's person, houses, papers and effects against unreasonable searches and seizures. Warrants are only valid with probable cause, signed by oath or affirmation, and particular about place, persons or things to be searched.

5) The right not to be a witness against oneself, not to be tried twice for the same crime, and there can be no capital punishment (death sentences) without calling a grand jury. There can be no deprivation of life, liberty or property without due process of law, nor private property taken for public use without due compensation.

6)   The right to a speedy, public trial in the district where the crime was committed, by a jury of one's peers, to be informed of the nature and cause of the accusation, to be confronted with witnesses, and to be able to call witnesses in one's favor, and the right to have the assistance of an attorney for defense.

7)   The right to trial by jury shall be preserved if the value in controversy exceeds twenty dollars. (Today that would be the equivalent of about $1000.00-2000.00). Also, one may not be tried twice for the same crime (also called double jeopardy).

8)   The right to reasonable bail, reasonable fines, and no cruel or unusual punishment (such as torture and police brutality).

9)   The enumeration of certain rights shall not be construed to deny or disparage others retained by the people.

10)   Powers not delegated to the federal government, nor prohibited by it to the states, are reserved to the states or the People.

The following are a few important comments about the American Bill of Rights.

THE SECOND AMENDMENT

John Adams, George Washington and others wrote that the most important of the ten Amendments was the second. As long as people can defend themselves and their property, the other rights have meaning. Confiscating guns places all the other rights in serious jeopardy. Most dictators take away the people's weapons. Soon afterwards, they impose a complete dictatorship. This occurred in Russia, Nazi Germany, England and elsewhere in the 20th century, and it continues to happen in other nations today.

The debate over gun rights is not about shooting rabbits or the safety of guns. Statistically, they are very safe, far safer for example than automobiles - or medical treatments. The real statistics about the horror of drug medicine is withheld from the people by skillful advertising and bending the truth. *The Second Amendment is about one's right to protect oneself and one's property - from all attackers, including the government.*

The right to defend oneself is the fundamental property right. Regardless of one's personal feeling about owning a gun, those who advocate altering the Second Amendment are enemies of liberty, no matter how well meaning they seem. Recently, England and Australia banned handguns. Crime rates have risen significantly. *Criminals love gun control.* It makes the people easy prey. Guns stop thousands of rapes, murders and robberies each year. This needs to be explained to everyone, everywhere.

WHY ISN'T FREEDOM OF HEALTH CARE IN THE BILL OF RIGHTS?

A *negative* right to health care is implied in the American federal Constitution. It means the right to seek health care wherever one wishes, from whomever one wishes. It does not mean free care, free drugs and free operations, which is definitely not in the US Constitution. That is properly termed *medical welfare.* The distinction is very important.

Did the founders of the country intend for the sovereign citizens to have freedom of choice in health care? I suggest the answer is yes. Here are several reasons for this. These reasons can help defend natural health care practices and practitioners.

- Private property rights are a basic concept in our legal tradition. What more important and intimate property does one have than one's body? Protection of one's property is a primary and logical right. It would make no sense that one could keep guns to protect oneself, for example, but should not be allowed to seek protection of the body against disease in the manner one chooses.

- The founders believed in a right to contract freely. Any contact between practitioner and client or patient implies a contract, no matter how informal. Article I, Section 10 of the federal Constitution states that "... No state shall pass any law impairing the obligation of contracts ...". All state constitutions contain a similar clause.

- Debate took place regarding inclusion of health care freedom in the Bill of Rights. Benjamin Rush, MD, the physician in charge of the Continental Army and a signer of the Declaration of Independence, warned:

"The Constitution of this republic should make special provision for medical freedom as well as religious freedom ... To restrict the art of healing to one class of men and deny equal privileges to others will constitute the Bastille of medical science. All such laws are unAmerican and despotic. They are fragments of the monarchy and have no place in a republic."

Some have called for a constitutional amendment regarding health care choice. However, this is a long and slow process.

DID THE FOUNDERS BELIEVE IN MEDICAL WELFARE?

While I cannot read the minds of the American founders, the following argue against this idea:

1. There was absolutely no discussion of it at the time.

2. It was not done at this time in history in any other nation, so there was no precedent.

3. Government medical welfare such as the current programs of Medicare and Medicaid violate the right to contract freely because they are mandatory. That is, everyone must pay for them, whether or not one participates.

4. There is no delegated authority to force these programs on the people of the 50 states. The American founders hated monopolies, which is what this amounts to.

5. These programs are riddled with fraud. Even without fraud they are financial disasters. Each year more rules are added, making them a paperwork nightmare for doctors and hospitals. Medicare rules currently fill 133,000 pages.

Private welfare societies, community health associations and churches used to provide medical welfare. They hired all types of healers and doctors to take care of their members. Pressure from the AMA put an end to community health associations early in the 20th century. The AMA did not like private welfare societies because they placed doctors on a fixed salary. Government welfare put the rest out of business.

A few private medical welfare systems remain, such as the excellent welfare systems of the Mormons, Catholics and Jewish groups in some areas of America and in other lands. However, they are under siege by the government welfare systems that compete directly with them.

13.
THE FORGOTTEN AMERICAN NINTH AMENDMENT

The Ninth Amendment to the US Constitution is an important one for lovers of freedom and liberty. Legal authorities generally ignored it until the last 40 years or so. The Ninth Amendment reads:

> "The enumeration in the Constitution, of certain rights, shall not be construed to deny or disparage others retained by the people."

The previous chapter explained that the Bill of Rights was simply a restatement of *some* of the rights retained by the people. The Ninth Amendment appears to confirm this view. It reminds the reader that just because some rights are enumerated, or listed in the Bill of Rights, does not mean there are no others. However, it does not state what these other rights are. This has been a source of legal debate for 200 years.

Two legal interpretations exist of the Ninth Amendment. One viewpoint is that the Ninth Amendment is *restrictive* only. In this view, James Madison, author of the Ninth Amendment, wanted the Ninth included because at the time certain states had bills of rights that were more extensive than the federal Bill of Rights. The contention is the Ninth Amendment was included so that the federal government could not infringe upon rights protected in state constitutions. In this view, the Ninth Amendment only restricts the federal government in relation to the states. It does not restrict state governments at all. This is the strict interpretation of the Ninth Amendment.

The opposing view is that the Ninth Amendment is not just a restrictive statement. It is a *declaratory* statement, pertaining to the future. It declares that rights that are not enumerated will be revealed and become apparent in the future. This view claims that it is in the spirit of the Constitution that other rights should be recognized and protected. Legal scholar Bennett Patterson wrote:

> "We will ultimately find that this Amendment is a succinct expression of the inherent dignity and liberty of the individual and a recognition of the soul of mankind, a belief in his spiritual nature and a humble acknowledgment of the infinity of our Creator and our nature ...
>
> As we become more civilized, we learn more about natural forces...such as steam and electricity. We also increase in spiritual and intellectual growth and are capable of understanding natural rights and liberties that have always existed, but which have been beyond our limited intellect to comprehend."
> (1)

This is the liberal or constructive interpretation of the Ninth Amendment.

COURT INTERPRETATION OF THE NINTH AMENDMENT

Early Supreme Court cases supported the restrictive interpretation of the Ninth Amendment. Until the nineteen sixties, a time of renewed interest in human rights, the Ninth Amendment received only minor commentary from judges and commentators. All this changed in 1965.

In Griswold v. Connecticut, the Supreme Court held unconstitutional Connecticut laws that criminalized the use of, or assistance in the use of, birth control. Justice Douglass wrote that the statutes violated the right of marital privacy created by specific guarantees in the First, Third, Fourth, Fifth and Ninth Amendments. This opinion by Justice Goldberg, joined by Chief Justice Warren and Justice Brennan, catapulted the Ninth Amendment into prominence. Justice Goldberg wrote that:

> "... the framers of the Constitution believed there are additional fundamental rights, protected from governmental infringement, which exist alongside those fundamental rights specifically mentioned in the first eight amendments...The Ninth Amendment, in indicating that not all such liberties are specifically mentioned in the first eight amendments, is surely relevant in showing the existence of other fundamental personal rights, now protected from state, as well as federal, infringement. In sum, the Ninth Amendment simply lends strong support to the view that the "liberty" protected by the Fifth and Fourteenth Amendments from infringement by the federal government or the states is not restricted to rights specifically mentioned in the first eight amendments." (2)

Since the Griswold case, the Ninth Amendment has been cited more than one thousand times. The most famous case was the Roe v. Wade decision on abortion. The Ninth Amendment was used to support the idea of a 'right of privacy'. Abortion was held to be a private matter. The government could not pass a law forbidding it.

The early intent of the Ninth Amendment was to protect the states and the people from federal encroachment. The recent use of the Ninth Amendment has been to nullify state laws, especially in the area of morals and sexual matters.

DOES THE NINTH AMENDMENT PROTECT JUST ANY RIGHT?

Raoul Berger, in the Cornell Law Review (3), sharply criticized Justice Goldberg for his interpretation of the Ninth Amendment in the Griswold case. Berger argued that if the Ninth Amendment can be used to protect some vague 'privacy right', what is to stop anyone from making up a right and then using the Ninth Amendment to protect it? Who is to say which rights will be protected? This is indeed a difficult question.

However, one can argue this is precisely the challenge of the law, to evolve as society evolves. It cannot remain static any more than technology, language, or culture remain static. Judge Goldberg and the other justices made their decision by referring to other provisions of the Constitution, to establish a framework or rationale for the unenumerated rights. Indeed, a right to privacy has a good constitutional foundation. It also dates back even further, to John Locke's theory that each person is basically his own master. Judge Cooley described this right as "the right to be let alone." (4)

THE NINTH AMENDMENT AND UNLICENSED HEALERS

I was unable to find evidence the Supreme Court ever took up the question of whether state medical practice acts violate a 'right to privacy', the right to associate and contract freely, or the right to protect one's bodily property. Until there is a definitive case, it remains an open question. I believe there is clearly a privacy issue involved in the right to offer and receive one's choice of services in health care, education, psychology and legal matters. Such services may be every bit as intimate and important as birth control or abortion.

NINTH AMENDMENT DECLARATIONS

A Ninth Amendment declaration sets forth that the service offered or received is a right retained by the people, since it is not a power given specifically to the government. Although not tested in court, I recommend that both practitioners and clients sign simple Ninth Amendment declarations.

One reason for this recommendation has to do with claiming rights. Also, it cannot hurt to do so, even if it is someday invalidated in court. Acting responsibly, particularly upon legal advice, lends substance to any action. Even if the Ninth Amendment declaration is invalidated in the future, one will have acted to the best of one's ability and this is a reasonable defense.

Also, one does not depend upon it alone. One uses the other forms discussed in chapter 5 to establish one's intent to practice responsibly.

Recently, the Supreme Court is favoring a right to privacy. The author feels that defending one's business in this manner is in accordance with the trend in interpretation of the Ninth Amendment.

For the client, a Ninth Amendment declaration can be part of a consent and disclaimer form. The practitioner keeps this on file. For the practitioner, the declaration should be filed with the County Recorder or Secretary of State, and a copy kept on file.

A Ninth Amendment declaration for a practitioner might read:

"Under Article Amendment IX of the Constitution of the United States of America, I, the undersigned, hereby declare and retain the God-given and natural right to:

1) Obtain an education from any institution or private school, including those whose views are different from orthodox or conventional thinking.

2) Practice nutrition counseling (or other work) for the benefit of my clients without being required to obtain a license from any government authority, and to do so in a manner consistent with my training and background.

3) Provide products and information for my clients consistent with my background and training."

Along with the Ninth Amendment declaration, one should add a 'constructive notice'. This states that a violation of one's Ninth Amendment right would entitle one to sue for violation of one's civil and constitutional rights. More complete statements for practitioners and clients are found in the last chapter of this book.

If some one or organization questions one's right to offer services, one would immediately send them a copy of the Ninth Amendment statement. Basically, one is claiming a right. Rights must be claimed. One is putting others on notice that one claims the right to practice under the Constitution. They are notified, in advance, that should they attempt to stop one, they may be in violation of the law. It shifts one from a defensive to an offensive position. It may also educate others regarding our rights under the Constitution.

NINTH AMENDMENT USE IN ARIZONA

Other uses exist for the Ninth Amendment. In 1990, the dietitians petitioned the Arizona state legislature for a licensing law. Part of a national effort by the American Dietetic Association, it would have given dietitians sole use of the word nutritionist. It was intended to set up a monopoly for offering nutrition services in the state. No need existed for such a license, as there were no complaints of harm in Arizona caused by nutritionists.

The bill sailed through two committees and appeared headed for passage by the full legislature. A group including myself consulted with Clinton Miller, a prominent health care lobbyist. In addition to organizing a phone and letter-writing campaign, we employed the Ninth Amendment.

Every practitioner, health food store, herb representative and others who would be affected by the new law signed a Ninth Amendment declaration and sent it to the Secretary of State and to their state legislators. It declared our right to offer nutrition services and to sell products, and if this right were violated, there could be lawsuits.

It is hard to assess the impact the Ninth Amendment declarations. However, within several days of filing the declarations, a legislative committee killed the dietitian's licensing bill by a vote of 10-0.

The above is a brief introduction to the Ninth Amendment. For those wishing to learn much more about it, an excellent book is *The Rights Retained By The People,* edited by Randy Barnett, published by George Mason University Press.

Notes

1. Patterson, B., "The Forgotten Ninth Amendment", The Rights Retained by the

People, ed. by Barnett, R., George Mason University Press, Fairfax, Virginia, 1989, p.113.

2. 381 U.S. at 492 (concurring opinion)

3. Berger, The Ninth Amendment, 66 Cornell Law Review, 1 (1980-81)

4. T. Cooley, Law of Torts 29 (2nd ed. 1888).

14.
IF LEGAL DISPUTES ARISE

In spite of safeguarding one's practice, legal challenges can still occur. This chapter offers suggestions for handling complaints and more serious legal difficulties. My personal experiences may serve as examples. Let us begin with common situations that can arise.

1) No One Is Perfect. One may unintentionally anger, inconvenience or even cause harm to another. Most clients will understand that one is human and occasionally makes mistakes. However, now and then a client is not so forgiving.

The best policy is *do not ignore complaints*. Call and acknowledge your awareness of the problem. Avoid becoming defensive or argumentative, as this can escalate into a legal problem. Apologize rapidly, whether or not one feels one did anything incorrect. Sometimes one is not aware of how a word or even a gesture affects another. A client who is ill or out of sorts can be extra sensitive to one's words or actions.

2) The Irate Family Member. One may work with a client professionally and adequately. However, a family member or friend who does not know what one does may blame one when the treatment outcome is not as desired. Usually this occurs when working with a client with a serious health condition. The client may be satisfied, but not a family member or well-meaning but upset friend.

This has occurred several times in my practice. The problems ended when I spoke directly with the family members. I reassured them I cared very much for the client's welfare and did my best. I avoided defensiveness, arguing or justifying my work and I reassured them I was available if other questions arose.

3) Quackbusters. Especially if one is in the vanguard of one's field, one may attract the wrath of another practitioner or an organization that seeks to stop innovation.

Several years ago, I rebutted an article written by a well-known quackbuster. His lawyer wrote a threatening letter demanding $2000.00 from me. If I did not pay, he would sue for libel as I had defamed the quackbuster in my article. I learned this individual wrote the same letter to many holistic practitioners to intimidate them. The quackbuster had no case, but I decided to hire an attorney to make sure things were handled correctly. Perhaps I could have ignored the threat. In general, however, it is best to answer all legal-sounding letters promptly.

Another time, an undercover police agent came to my office posing as a client. By avoiding the words diagnose, treat and cure, and avoiding improper administrative procedures, no harm to me resulted. It is best to be prepared as one never knows who will come through the door.

4) Employees And Others. Disputes can often arise with employees, associates, landlords, vendors, suppliers, or total strangers with whom one may become involved in one's business.

Twice, letting employees go resulted in ill feelings on their part. One threatened me with legal action, claiming I owed her money. She had little grounds for complaint. However, after consulting an attorney, I paid her a small sum rather than risk a problem. She and the other employee later apologized.

PREVENTION

If a situation does not feel right, wait and reflect before continuing. A client who starts describing how he sued another practitioner, for example, may be best referred to someone else. Also, consider not taking care of or referring out any clients who seem mentally very unbalanced or very hostile. I have a strict rule that I will not work with anyone who speaks abusively to my secretaries or staff.

When speaking, and particularly when writing, always double check facts, do not exaggerate, and be careful about naming names and saying anything that could be construed as a personal accusation. A forgiving attitude is always better than placing blame and denouncing others, no matter what one believes they have done.

In today's litigious climate, go slowly when becoming involved with people one does not know. This includes employees, associates, landlords and everyone else. *Always put agreements in writing.* This does not mean one is suspicious, just wise. Be suspicious of someone who does not wish to put an agreement in writing.

Contracts can be simple. Use plain English and show contracts to a lawyer or another trained in reading contracts. There are many ways to write a contract or agreement.

RESPONDING TO COMPLAINTS

Complaints against you may include personal letters, letters to the editor, letters to the state attorney general, complaints to your professional organization, attempts to extort money, other legal threats, or actual filing of a lawsuit.

Each needs to be handled appropriately. For example, a personal letter from an unsatisfied client may not require an answer. *As a general rule, however, any complaint should be answered promptly.* Failure to do so may be seen as irresponsibility or acknowledgment of guilt. A rapid and thorough response may also help diffuse a possible legal problem.

If a legal-sounding letter has been received, it may be best not to talk directly to the other party, especially if one is angry or upset. When the quackbuster accused me of slander, I phoned him. When he heard who I was, I heard a tape recorder click on. I realized he could use anything I might say against me and I hung up immediately and instead called an attorney. So be careful!

When responding to letters in writing, maintain one's composure and answer directly. Sarcasm, anger, fear and other emotional responses serve no purpose. Always wait a day or two and then reread your letter before sending it. Even better, have an uninvolved friend or an excellent attorney help you respond in the best way.

ATTORNEYS

First, if one needs legal assistance, find someone who knows how to handle the type of problem one is having. It may be an attorney, but it could be someone else. A professional organization may offer legal services or can direct one to an appropriate person. Attorneys specialize. If necessary, ask any lawyer for a referral.

Schedule an initial consultation to evaluate the attorney. Bring all relevant paperwork, including a copy of any written complaint, and the client's records. The attorney also needs to know what kinds of insurance you have, including, of course, malpractice insurance if you have it.

Arrange this material ahead of time so you can present it clearly and concisely. As with going to a doctor, do not diagnose the problem oneself. Allow the lawyer to make his assessment.

Be clear about a attorney's charges. Ask about hourly fees, retainers, court costs, filing costs, and fees for copying, phone calls and more. Lawyers tend to charge for everything!

Settling a dispute out of court is always best, and should always be tried first. Avoid attorneys who want to go to court first. If one is not satisfied with the legal advice one receives, get a second opinion from another attorney or experienced person. Most communities have many attorneys to choose from.

FINAL WORDS

When a legal problem develops, if possible do not worry about or resent it. Welcome the opportunity to extend love rather than projecting anger or fear. One should not have many legal challenges if one follows the suggestions in this book. If one has a large practice or is visible in the community, one is more of a target. This is part of life, especially in America today.

One will become stronger and wiser by handling difficulties properly. By all means, do not let irrational fears hold one back from doing what is wise and beneficial for clients. This book began with the premise that one is here to extend love to others through a professional practice. If a legal dispute arises, do what needs to be done. However, for one's own sake choose to extend love and forgiveness no matter what.

Act with courage, dignity and a forgiving attitude. Check one's motives to see that one's ego is not in the way. However, continuously questioning motives is not helpful. I believe that higher forces are in charge. Have faith and ask for guidance that is for the highest good for all involved. If one is meant to continue extending love through the offering of services and one sticks with one's principles, the outcome will be positive.

15.
THE FULLY INFORMED JURY

If a legal difficulty arises, avoid going to court if at all possible. It is a jungle! The outcome is not at all assured, no matter how clear the case. However, should it be necessary, it would be helpful to have *a fully informed jury of one's peers.* This short chapter may be an eye opener.

The Magna Charta, in 1215, established a clear principle of English and American law. In criminal cases, it is the right and duty of the jury to judge not only the facts of a case, namely whether the accused broke the law. *They were also to judge the validity of the law itself.* The jury may acquit the accused either because he did not break the law, or because the law itself is unfair or otherwise faulty. This dual role for the jury is sometimes called *the power of jury nullification.* That is, the jury has the power to nullify the law itself. A little reflection will show this dual power of the jury is essential:

> "If the jury have no right to judge of the justice of a law of the government, then plainly, they can do nothing to protect the people against the oppressions of the government; for there are no oppressions which the government may not authorize by law." - from *An Essay on the Trial by Jury* (1852) by Lysander Spooner.

"It is presumed, that juries are the best judges of facts; it is, on the other hand, presumable, that the courts are the best judges of the law. But still both objects are within your power of decision. You have a right to take upon yourselves to judge both, and to determine the law as well as the facts in controversy."

- Instructions to the jury given by John Jay, chief justice, in the first case tried before the Supreme Court of the United States, *State of Georgia v. Brailsford*, 3 Dall I, 1794.

"There is the existence of an unreviewable and irreversible power in the jury, to acquit, in disregard of the instructions on the law ..." US v. Dougherty, 473 F2d 1113, pg.1132 (1972).

"The verdict, therefore, stands conclusive and unquestionable, in both law and fact ... it may be said that juries have a power and legal right to pass upon both the law and the fact." Sparf v. U.S., 156 US 51, pg 80, 15 Sup. Ct. 273, pg 285.

The jury was to be the final arbiter of the law. It matters not if the legislature passes laws. If a jury declares the law unjust or not in conformity with the Constitution, the law is of no effect. Once again, the intent was to give ultimate power to the citizens, not to judges or legislators.

LOSS OF THE POWER OF THE JURY

The power of the jury has been severely curtailed over the years. Today, one often hears on the news that a judge refused to allow certain testimony, or refused to allow the jury to consider certain issues. The judge often tells the jury exactly upon what they can and cannot base their decision. This is far from a fully informed jury. It is also improper! *For the record, jurors may not be punished for anything they say in the sanctity of a deliberation room or for any decision they make.*

Also, attorneys today are usually able to disqualify and thereby get rid of any juror who thinks independently or who might be a problem for him or her to convince (or brainwash). This, too, is an abomination and an abuse of the jury system.

Finally, in many cases in our courts today, there is no jury at all and judges alone try the case. This also goes against the founding principles of the nation that everyone is entitled to a trial by a jury of one's peers provided it is an important matter.

The jury system, a potent safeguard of our liberty, is in serious disarray. It is also possible that there is a problem with the concept of jury nullification.

WHAT IF THE JURY NULLIFIES A GOOD LAW?

A jury could nullify a law that is helpful, but the jury does not like it, such as marijuana prohibition at the federal level, or they don't understand the law. This is the potential difficulty with the idea of jury nullification.

In this case, the prosecutors or opposition could file an appeal, or ask that the law be rewritten. However, this takes time, during which a dangerous or objectionable behavior would be allowed, presumably. It is true that a judge can issue a stay or injunction against the person until the next trial, perhaps, but this may not happen.

One can argue that this is preferable to convicting a person of a crime because the jury is not allowed to judge the validity of a bad law. In this case, the person can appeal the decision.

However, this is costly and often the person loses his home, his business and perhaps more than this for several years until the appeal occurs.

I must assume that the founders of America, and indeed those who wrote the Magna Charta, thought of this objection, and decided to err on the side of the citizens and against the government, which has far more power and financial means at their disposal. In most cases, this is undoubtedly true. However, the issue as to whether the benefits of a fully informed jury outweigh the dangers may need more study and research.

THE FULLY INFORMED JURY AMENDMENT

The *Fully Informed Jury Association* is an organization seeking to remedy the jury situation. They have an excellent website that explains the rights of jurors. They also propose an Amendment to the federal Constitution entitled the Fully Informed Jury Amendment. It would require judges to inform juries that they are empowered to judge not only the facts of their case, but also the law itself. It would return power to the citizens and reduce the tyranny of judges and lawyers.

I recommend this organization very strongly. The website is also excellent to check if you are called for jury duty. For more information, call 1-800-835-5879 and visit **www.fija.org**.

16.
FORMS

This chapter offers sample forms for disclosure, consent and disclaimer statements for your clients. Also presented are sample Ninth Amendment Declarations for clients and for the practitioner.

In addition, I have included a Constructive Notice. This is a warning or advanced notice that anyone interfering with your work is subject to prosecution for violation of your clients' or your rights. The words 'under the color of law' means under the pretense or the appearance of law.

The Ninth Amendment Declaration and Constructive Notice are less necessary unless you are interested in the Ninth Amendment. The Ninth Amendment forms are modified from samples courtesy of Mr. Conrad LeBeau, who has worked with the Ninth Amendment for some 15 years. Several other model forms were also reviewed to arrive at the samples below.

I also included a basic employment contract. I strongly suggest using this if you have employees, both to avoid disputes and improve your communication with employees.

Modify these forms for your own practice. Hopefully, the information in this book will allow you to do so without losing the spirit and intent of the form. Remember, keep it simple and keep your language clear and readable.

Here are sample forms for the client to fill out and sign:

SAMPLE FORMS:

CONSENT, DISCLOSURE AND DISCLAIMER FORM

I request that (practitioner name) perform (your procedure, evaluation, therapy, etc.) and set up a program (or have sessions, etc.) for the purpose of (reducing stress, enhancing health, improving well-being, etc.).

I understand that (practitioner name) has a (certification, degree or training) from (name of school), an accredited school in x state (you may also add other qualifications such as years of experience).

I understand that x therapy is not intended as diagnosis, prescription, or treatment for any disease, physical or mental. It is also not intended as a substitute for regular medical care.

NINTH AMENDMENT DECLARATION

ARTICLE IX, U.S. CONSTITUTION
"The enumeration in the Constitution, of certain rights, shall not be construed to deny or disparage others retained by the People."

Under the Ninth Amendment to the Constitution of the United States of America, I retain the right to freedom of choice in health care (or psychological services, or educational services, etc...). This includes the right to choose my diet, and to obtain, purchase and use any therapy, regimen, modality, remedy or product recommended by the therapist, doctor or any practitioner of my choice.

The enumeration in this declaration of these rights shall not be construed to deny or disparage other rights retained by me, or my right to amend this declaration at any time.

CONSTRUCTIVE NOTICE

Notice is hereby given to any person who receives a copy of this Declaration and who, acting under the color of law, intentionally interferes with the free exercise of the rights retained by me under the Ninth Amendment, as enumerated in this declaration, that they may be in violation of my civil and constitutional rights, Title 42, U.S.C. 1983 et seq. and Title 18, Section 241.

Date:_____   Signed_____

Be sure your client signs these forms.

The practitioner may also sign a Ninth Amendment Declaration declaring the right to offer services, and a Constructive Notice as well. These are provided below. You may send a copy of these to the Secretary of State's office.

PROVIDERS DECLARATION OF NINTH AMENDMENT RIGHTS

ARTICLE IX, U.S. CONSTITUTION
"The enumeration in the Constitution, of certain rights, shall not be construed to deny or disparage others retained by the People."

I, the undersigned, hereby declare and retain the following natural and God-given rights under Article Amendment IX of the Constitution of the United States of America:

1) The right to obtain an education from any institution or private school, including those whose views are different from conventional practice of healing, (or education, etc.)

2) The right to practice nutrition counseling (or other work) for the benefit of my clients without being required to obtain a license from any governmental authority, and to do so in a manner consistent with my training and background. My training and background are ....

3) The right to provide products, regimens, modalities and services to anyone for any benefit or purpose providing:

a. I shall not provide any service that I am not qualified to provide based on my experience and education;

b. I shall make no false representation(s) about my education and training experience;

c. I shall make no intentionally exaggerated, false or misleading claims for the health products and services that I provide;

d. I shall inform any one(s) to whom I provide products and services when the protocol or regiment is experimental;

e. I shall avoid claiming that someone was "cured" of an illness unless the disease remains in remission for five years or longer;

f. All person(s) will be advised in a "Client Request and Authorization Form" to seek a second evaluation from a medical doctor, unless they have already done so.

4) I retain the right to provide customer references upon request.

5) I retain the right to use testimonials.

6) I retain the right to provide information on the intended purposes and benefits of my products and services. The health and well-being of my clients shall by my sole concern. All clients will be given a copy of this Health Care Provider's Notice at the time of initial consultation.

7) All rights retained herein are declared retroactive to the date of my 18th birthday.

The enumeration, in this declaration, of these rights shall not be construed to deny or disparage others retained by me, or my right to amend this declaration at any time. These rights, which are asserted for reasonable and good cause, are declared to be retained by the people under the Ninth Amendment to the Constitution, all state and federal laws to the contrary notwithstanding. In any litigation brought by any party objecting to the rights declared herein, a jury, representing the people, shall have the right to modify, nullify, or expand upon the Ninth Amendment rights claimed in this document.

Notice is hereby given to any person(s) who, acting under the color of law, intentionally interferes with the free exercise of the rights retained by me under the Ninth Amendment, as enumerated in this declaration, that they may be in violation of my civil and constitutional rights, Title 42, U.S.C. 1983 et seq. and Title 18, Section 241.

Date:_____   Signed:_____

Notary:

The form signed by the client should be kept on file by the practitioner. The form for the practitioner is to be signed in front of a notary and sent to your county recorder, secretary of state or any other authorities you may feel appropriate. Keep a copy in your files. (Sovereigns who file statements with any recording agency of the government must include a statement that this is for recording purposes only, not for entry into a foreign jurisdiction.)

SAMPLE EMPLOYMENT CONTRACT

Another useful form to clarify your relationship with employees and protect yourself legally is an employment contract. It need not be long and complex. It is a very wise idea. Here is a sample of what it needs to include at the minimum:

Employee Name_____   **Date**_____

I. Job Title:

II. Job Description:

III. List Of Work Duties: (List many, such as answering phones, scheduling appointments, taking messages, greeting clients, filing, typing letters, taking notes, selling products, bookkeeping, maintaining product inventory, managing the front office, etc.

IV. Wages or salary: (Include starting salary, the plan for raises, work hours and times, and overtime hours if applicable.)

VI. Benefits:
1. Paid holidays (such as Christmas and Thanksgiving)
2. Unpaid holidays and vacations (when, how often, how much notice needed)
3. Medical benefits or insurance if you offer it.
4. Other fringe benefits. (These may be product discounts or therapy discounts, free consultations or other benefits you would offer.)

V. Probationary Period And Evaluations: (Very important – employees need feedback and the boss needs to be able to evaluate the employee as well. A six-month probation period is good.)

VI. Termination of Employment: (It might read something like: employer and employee agree to give each other 3 weeks verbal and written notice of the need to terminate employment.)

Signatures: Employee_____   **Employer**_____

CONCLUSION

The law as it relates to unlicensed practitioners is evolving. There is a great need to return to basic legal principles that were established at the founding of the American nation and have been adopted to varying extents by other nations.

The topic of restoring the Constitution is controversial, and we have only scratched the surface of the issue. Hopefully, it has whetted your appetite for further study. The present level of understanding on this issue among the population is dismal. Perhaps you will help educate others.

Keeping one's intent pure, maintaining high integrity, treating people with kindness and consideration, and using common sense are the most important aspects of avoiding legal difficulties. The material in this book provides added legal protection, but is no substitute for thinking and acting correctly. Focus on extending love rather than projecting fear. An attitude of forgiveness toward everyone, and asking only how one can be of help, keeps one properly focused and helps greatly to stay out of harm's way. I wish you much joy and success in all your endeavors.

ORGANIZATIONS AND BIBLIOGRAPHY

1. American Association for Health Freedom, (800) 230-2762, www.healthfreedom.net. An excellent lobbying group for health freedom.

2. American Health Legal Foundation, 1601 N. Tucson Blvd, Ste. 9, Tucson, AZ 85716 (800) 635-1196. Excellent group, associated with the American Association of Physicians and Surgeons, helps preserve private practice of medicine in America.

3. The Foundation of Economic Education, 30 South Broadway Irvington-on-Hudson, New York, 10533, www.fee.org, (800) 960-4FEE. Publishes an excellent monthly magazine and seminars teaching principles of liberty.

4. Fully Informed Jury Association, PO Box 5570, Helena, M T 59604-5570, www.fija.org, (800) 835-5879. This group is dedicated to returning the full power of jury nullification to the people of America. See Chapter 15.

5. Future of Freedom Foundation, 11350 Random Hills Road, #800, Fairfax, VA, www.fff.org, (703) 934-6101. An uncompromising freedom group.

6. HealthKeepers Alliance, 3 Church Circle, #100, Annapolis, MD 21401, (888) 965-5005, www.healthkeeps.net. Health freedom group that presents a health freedom expo.

7. National Health Federation, P. O. Box 688, Monrovia, CA 91017, (626) 357-2181, www.thenhf.com. This is the oldest health freedom organization. They do wonderful work to preserve health freedom on many fronts.

8. National Center for Constitutional Studies, c/o PO Box 37110, Washington, District of Columbia Near PZ [20013] (202) 371-0008. Good information about our Constitution.

9. The Institute For Health Freedom, 1825 Eye Street, N,W, Ste. 400, Washington, DC, 20006, (202) 429-6610, www.ForHealthFreedom.org. Excellent information source.

10. The Institute For Justice, 901 N. Glebe Road, Ste. 900, Arlington, VA 22203, www.ij.org, (703) 682-9320. A wonderful group of attorneys who help abolish occupational licensing laws of all kinds, without charge.

BIBLIOGRAPHY

1. Andrews, L.B., "The Shadow Health Care System: Regulation of Alternative Health Care Providers", Houston Law Review, Vol. 32, #5, Symposium 1996. (many references).
2. Andrews, L.B., *Deregulating Doctoring: Do Medical Licensing Laws Meet Today's Health Care Needs?* People's Medical Society, 1983, 1986.
3. *Dissent in Medicine*, Contemporary Books, Inc., Chicago, 1985.
4. Green, J., "Medicine and the Scope of Practice Boundaries", The Townsend Letter for Doctors, Feb/Mar 1995, #139-140, pp.79-82.
5. *History of American Constitutional Or Common Law*, The Message Company, c/o RR 2, Box 307 MM, Santa Fe, New Mexico state Near PZ [87505].
6. Lebeau, C., *Ninth Amendment Defense Kit*, P.O. Box 164, S74W17000,JanesvilleRd, Muskego, WI 53150. (414) 679-1846.
7. March, R., *The Fundamental Teachings of American Liberty*, 1994, House of Common Law Press, c/o 9450 E. Becker, Ste. 2006, Scottsdale, Arizona state Near PZ [85260]. (602) 314-1465. (House of Common Law Press offers other excellent books.)

INDEX